THE JESUS SYSTEM
HEALING. RESTORATION.
GOD'S LOVE.

JUSTIN J. PETRICK
RENEE A. PETRICK

Scripture quotations marked NIV are taken from the HOLY BIBLE, NEW INTERNATIONAL VERSION ®. Copyright © 1973, 1978, 1984 by International Bible Society. Used by permission of Zondervan. All rights reserved.
Scripture quotations marked KJV are taken from the Holy Bible, King James Authorized Version, which is in the public domain.
Scripture quotations marked YLT are taken from the Holy Bible, Young's Literal Translation, which is in the public domain.
All scripture emphasis my own.
Unless otherwise specified, Hebrew and Greek translations taken from blueletterbible.com

THE JESUS SYSTEM:
Healing. Restoration. God's Love.
1st Edition

ISBN-13: 978-1717012746
ISBN-10: 1717012744

Printed in the United States of America
© 2018 by Justin J. Petrick & Renee A. Petrick

Petrick Ministries
A division of Mizpah, Inc.
10813 Fillmore St. NE
Blaine, MN 55449
petrickministries@hotmail.com

DEDICATION

To my wife, my best friend forever, my soul mate, my better half, the love of my life. Your love for Jesus is inspirational, your heart pure, your mind beautiful, your nature and character full of dignity, strength, wisdom, faith, compassion, and love. I could not have done this without your support, your prayers, your endless hours of editing, and most importantly, your love for Jesus. I love you.

To my daughters, I love you always and forever.

To my mom, thankful for your unconditional love, prayers, and never giving up on me.

Ross and Sheryl, Pastor Nate Ruch, and Pastor Tom Belt, grateful more than you will ever know for your support and encouragement.

And special thanks to Lisa and Dewey, Megan Finsel, Suzanne Oyebola, and Marie Boggess for your work and investment in what God has laid on our hearts.

ABOUT THE AUTHORS

Justin J. Petrick is a Firefighter-Paramedic with a BS in Psychology and Family Social Sciences from the University of Minnesota. After living a life in the bondage of addictions for over 20 years that originated from an abusive childhood, Justin woke up on November 8th, 2012 experiencing God's presence and love that supernaturally healed and radically transformed his life in a single night. Despite not seeking God nor desiring Him in his life, Justin was not only healed but was also given an intense passion and desire to know God. Justin craved to seek God and His Word to understand this presence and love that saturated his very being, making him whole and complete in Christ. After spending years asking God, "What happened?" The Jesus System was His answer.

Renee, a teacher with a BS in Psychology and Bible from Northwestern University, grew up in a Christian home. It wasn't until age 17 that she completely surrendered her life to Jesus. God spoke a simple word to her heart that would guide and protect her as she would wait and prepare for her husband: "Do not settle. Position yourself with me. Allow me to make your life a gift". Renee took this word deeply to heart, fixed her eyes on Jesus, and trusted that as she sought Him first everything else would follow (Matthew 6:33). She resolved that He would bring the right man, at the right time, and in the right way. After thirteen years, Renee kept her vow and God kept His promise. Prior to meeting Justin, Renee's heart broke from striving to earn God's love for over a decade. This mentality was internally exhausting and almost took her life. Renee overcame depression and suicidal ideation by eradicating her inaccurate beliefs about God's nature and character, replacing them with the truth and life of His Word. God individually made their hearts whole with the revelation of His perfect and unconditional love.

Justin's and Renee's revelation of God's perfect love is the catalyst for the Jesus System. This revelation of God's perfect love has ignited a passion to teach accurate theology about the true nature and character of God. What is believed in the heart is lived out in this life. A solid foundation of the finished works of Jesus Christ opens the door to experiencing the love God intended for all humankind.

God is no respecter of persons, what He has done for one He will do for all. In God's unconditional love we are made complete where nothing is missing, and nothing is lacking. Justin and his wife, Renee, have a passion to inspire belief in a personal God by teaching His Word, the gospel of the grace of Jesus Christ, and through sharing their experiences of being set free from their own personal bondages by the life-giving love, power, and presence of the Holy Spirit.

Acts 20:24 (KJV): But none of these things move me, neither count I my life dear unto myself, so that I might finish my course with joy, and the ministry, which I have received of the Lord Jesus, to testify the gospel of the grace of God.

FROM THE AUTHORS

Greetings! My wife and I are so blessed that you have chosen to take this journey through The Jesus System with us. We believe it will truly impact your life through bringing intimacy into your relationship with our Lord and Savior, Jesus Christ. Our relationship with Him is an ever-increasing experience. There is no limit to where God can take us, not only in this life with Him but also within His presence and love.

The Bible says that we can only worship God in spirit and truth (John 4:24). God breathes to life our spirit upon salvation, but we must pursue the truth for ourselves with the guidance and wisdom of the Holy Spirit. We cannot worship what we do not know or do not understand. This is what challenges most believers, new and mature, in that our relationship and intimacy with God is directly related to our accurate knowledge of the truth of His Word. It is our desire to bring this truth of God's nature and character, or His Word, to you, to make it the foundation of your life with a perfect and loving God.

This book is living and interactive, meaning it will reveal different truths to different people even while catering to the different seasons of life we go through. As we apply His Word to each aspect of our lives, each of us will experience different areas of transformation in life as the Holy Spirit leads and develops us. Keep in mind, this will take time. For some, it will take weeks or months to process all the information in this book while applying it to life experiences. Others may have to read sections of this book over a time or two for it to fully bear fruit in life. And for others, it will radically change deep seated beliefs, completely changing how they see and interact with God immediately.

Because this book is so scripturally based, uniquely deep, and challenging, each time you go through this book, new revelations of the truth of God's nature, character, and love for you will surface. The Holy Spirit is our teacher, instructor, and counselor. He takes the number one role in this book by revealing the nature of God's perfect love for us, through His Word, individually and specifically.

As you go through this book, I encourage you to fervently press into the Holy Spirit, being sensitive to what He would teach you through not only this book, but more importantly through your individual, personal time reading the Bible. As you go through this study along with your individual, personal devotion with God, watch His empowerment take fruit in your life. Seek Him first in all you do, and all things will be added unto you (Matthew 6:33)!

Before we get started, you may be asking "Why a systems approach?" Does God relate to us on a systematic level? No. A systems approach is for our benefit in helping us understand the whole picture of life and nothing more. General Systems Theory is a science of wholeness, developed in 1936 by an Austrian biologist

Ludwig von Bertalanffy. General Systems Theory helps us understand that a person's life can be broken down into parts, or subsystems, and are more valuable when they are interconnected, functioning harmoniously as a whole. Life is a system that has many components that together, as a whole, make up reality. Therefore, the understanding of life is only possible through viewing it as a whole.

General Systems Theory also shows us that the output, or the way our life currently exists, is a result of the way our life, or system, has been set up. In other words, life will produce what it has been designed to produce. This is saying that when an event happens in life, good or bad despite what we may think, there is no single cause but rather multiple influences by multiple parts, or systems, of our life. For example, we think that a new, better paying job will solve our problems in life. When, in reality, there are multiple influences creating the problem, such as our spending habits, how we view ourselves, and the power we give money through our beliefs, not just the job itself. When trying to understand life experiences, or solve its problems, we minimize or limit our view through believing life happens in single cause-and-effect relationships. In other words, we think problems arise from one area of life rather than understanding that problems or experiences occur through the influence of multiple parts, or systems, generating the problem as a whole. This is why eradication problems or habits in life is so difficult, in that they are often enmeshed through every part of our life.

It is difficult to see life as a whole because of how complex these interconnections are between the different systems of our life and their influence on one another. We live in a society that is ingrained in thinking of relationships purely through a cause-and-effect lens that impairs or limits our understanding of life as a whole. In using a 'system' as a metaphor in viewing life, one has the ability to restructure each part, or system, of life in God's Word, therefore producing a life of intimacy with God. When each part of our life is rooted in God's perfect love, the result will be a reality that is lived in God's perfect love. This happens because problems, or barriers to experiencing intimacy with God, will be eradicated in not just one part of life, but through area of our life, thus effecting the whole. This happens naturally through laying the foundation of each part of our life, our systems of Belief, Faith, Identity, Communication, and Network, in the truth of God's Word. The end result will be a life that is stable, interconnected, functioning harmoniously as a whole in God's perfect love.

TABLE OF CONTENTS

CHAPTER 1

BELIEFS

1.1 LIFE IS ABOUT RELATIONSHIPS

The Jesus System has been created based on the principles of General Systems Theory, a theory that is often summed up by Aristotle's quote, "The whole is greater than the sum of its parts." General Systems Theory shows us that the understanding of life is only possible through viewing it as a whole. This science of wholeness not only gives us the ability to understand the parts of our life as independent, self-sustaining systems that interact with one another, but that they are more valuable when interconnected, functioning harmoniously as a whole. To see life as a whole, we will break down our life into five parts or systems. They are:

1. Beliefs
2. Faith
3. Identity
4. Communication
5. Network

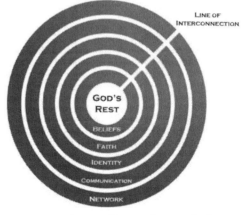

By separately establishing each part, or system, of life in God's Word, a life fully interconnected in the Word of God will be revealed, functioning harmoniously as a whole in God's perfect love.

Establishing life in harmony with God's Word will change how we view relationships. A life rooted in God's Word will influence how we think about ourselves and others, how we communicate with ourselves and others, how we view ourselves and others and, specifically in this study, how we see ourselves in relationship with Jesus Christ.

Fully understanding life in Christ will be life-changing. We are designed and created to not only live in relationship with God, but also to give and receive the love of Christ from one another as a means to fulfill the greatest need of our being: To establish a sense of meaning and purpose, or in other words, self-worth. Nothing is more influential to our self-worth than our belief in a loving God and our relationship with Him.

Beliefs are used to understand experiences which guide us into meaning and satisfaction, or lack thereof, through relationships. Our perceptual lens, which is made up of beliefs, thoughts, feelings, and experiences, determines reality. Our self-worth is based on this perceived reality.

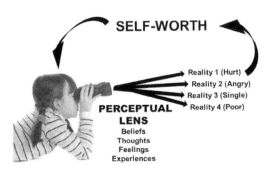

APPLICATION

Have you wondered why one day you can feel on top of the world and the next it seems as if nothing is going right? Reality changes according to our perception, which changes according to our beliefs, thoughts, feelings, and experiences. Thus, our view of life can change in an instant. And just like our perception determines our reality, the reality we perceive determines our self-worth.

"Each of us has a variety of [beliefs] we use to explain [experiences]; our personal [beliefs] are our guides as we move towards greater meaning and satisfaction in our lives."
– Bateson (1972)

Our focus (perceptual lens) on experiences leads to thoughts which leads to feelings and emotions. Feelings and emotions that are experienced long enough will become beliefs of our heart and, when negative, can be referred to as a broken heart.

It is imperative for beliefs to be established in the Word of God to align our understanding of life experiences to the Word of God (Psalm 119:144, Matthew 6:33, Hebrews 4:12). There is no greater way to explain and understand life, therefore who we are, than through the Word of God. The author of the Bible is not only the author of truth and life, but the author and creator of our very being.

There is no greater way to explain and understand life, therefore who we are, than through the Word of God. The author of the Bible is not only the author of truth and life, but the author and creator of our very being.

Problems in life arise when our beliefs (thoughts) are not aligned to the Word of God (Romans 12:2). Inaccurate beliefs about God and how He relates to life will lead us astray and continually compound our diversion from Christ. This will lead to a Christian life that simply 'isn't working'; a life with Christ that lacks results and is filled with confusion, despair, and frustration (Galatians 3:1, 1 Corinthians 14:33).

When our beliefs are based on God's Word, our reality becomes filled with His truth and life. This enables us to see reality as God does, resulting in seeing ourselves as God does— whole and complete in Christ. Seeing reality through a lens based on God's Word produces a stable, constant source of self-worth through

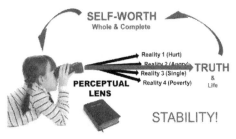

His perfect love for us because our perception of reality will not change with the feelings and emotions that can often rule life.

The purpose of this study is to change our perceptual lens, therefore reality, by rooting our beliefs in the truth and life of God's Word, thus revealing the whole picture of living everyday life in God's perfect love.

1.2 THE POWER OF BELIEFS

When our beliefs do not line up with the Word of God they will blind us to His nature and character, therefore how He relates to everyday life.

Theology means the study and understanding of God. We create inaccurate theology when we do not understand God's nature, character, and how He relates to everyday life. Simply put, without accurately understanding God's Word, we will make up our version of God based on our interpretation of life's experiences and how we think He relates to them. Inaccurate theology or inaccurate beliefs are created to make sense of experiences when we do not understand how God relates to life.

> Inaccurate beliefs are created to make sense of experiences when we do not understand how God relates to life.

Let us look at this picture, for example. Who do you see?

A young girl or an old woman?

If you look closely, the picture is both a young and old woman depending on what you focus on. Now that you have identified both, test yourself on how fast you can switch your perception between the two. That is how fast our brain can switch its perception of reality based on what we believe!

Beliefs lead to a behavioral response as a reaction to the perception of an experience we are having. The mind can change one's current perception of reality in an instant, and in so doing, alter one's behavior. All it takes is for our focus to switch. The scary thing is, the beliefs that alter our perception of reality, or what influences whether we see the old or young woman for example, may not even be our own beliefs.

"Our most private thoughts and emotions are not actually our own, for we think in terms of languages and images which we did not invent, but which were given to us by society." - Watts, 1972, p.64

The reason God says to seek Him first (Matthew 6:33) is because He knows the influence of the world on our perception of reality. In fact, society is the number one source of influence on behaviors through the knowledge and beliefs it ingrains in us when we are not rooted in the truth of God's Word. When society teaches what is right and wrong, what is and is not acceptable, we are learning what is called social constructions, or society's 'made-up' knowledge.

THINKING POINT

The social constructions of the religious leaders, or their inaccurate beliefs, caused them to have a false perception of reality in that they missed the identity of Jesus as the Messiah, despite anticipating his coming for centuries. This is one of the reasons the Pharisees rejected Jesus, leading to His crucifixion (Luke 22-23). In fact, the Pharisees were so blinded by their inaccurate beliefs that they accused Jesus, who was doing nothing but healing people I might add, as being demon-possessed (John 8:52). Jesus was hated without cause (Psalm 69).

John 8:52 (NIV): At this they exclaimed, "Now we know that you are demon-possessed!"

Here are a couple examples of social constructions or society's 'made-up' knowledge:

1. Gender specific toys: Children don't learn which toys are for girls and which toys are for boys through objective experience, but rather through what society teaches them as normal.
2. Racism: There is no biological reason for racism to exist other than it was generated by some to suppress a group of people by their race or ethnicity. Science has proven there are greater variances of individual differences within races than between races. In other words, there is one race: The human race.

A Biblical example of society's 'made-up' knowledge is John 9:1-2, when the disciples thought a man was born blind because of sin.

> **Inaccurate beliefs about God are one of, if not the most, damaging influence and primary reason why a person fails to experience a life lived in God's perfect love.**

Inaccurate beliefs about God are one of, if not the most, damaging influence and primary reason why a person fails to experience a life lived in God's perfect love.

The goal of this study is to identify and deconstruct inaccurate beliefs, ideologies, values, which are the motivators of behavior, that are not aligned with the Word of God. Only then can we replace them with the truth and life of God's Word (2 Corinthians 10:5).

When we replace inaccurate beliefs with the truth of God's Word, a reality of intimacy is produced with God because we will understand the magnitude of His love for us, thus changing our motivators of behavior.

Behavioral change is a natural result of experiencing God's perfect love and is different from change by behavioral modification through willpower.

> *Romans 3:22 (KJV): Even the righteousness of God which is by faith of Jesus Christ unto all and upon all them that believe: for there is no difference:*

Many people try to 'will' righteous behavior through their effort, but this route will always fail. The ten commandments revealed to us that we would never be able to 'will' righteous behavior through being perfectly obedient to the law. If we could, we would not need Jesus as our Savior, or the Cross, because we would be able to obtain righteousness ourselves. There are 2 ways to righteousness. One is through the law or through our own ability to keep the law, the other is through faith.

2 WAYS TO RIGHTEOUSNESS

Behavioral Modification Through Willpower

Decision-Making

Righteous Behavior

Righteousness Through Belief
Romans 3:22-24

Righteousness through the law:

Galatians 3:10-11 (NIV): For all who rely on the works of the law are under a curse, as it is written: "Cursed is everyone who does not continue to do everything written in the Book of the law".

Righteousness through Grace:

*Romans 3:22-24 (NIV): "This righteousness is **given through faith** in Jesus Christ to all who believe. There is no difference between Jew and Gentile, (23) for all have sinned and fall short of the glory of God, (24) and all are justified **freely** by his grace through the redemption that came by Christ Jesus."*

Just like our faith and belief in Jesus Christ is the catalyst for our salvation, our faith and beliefs are the catalysts for our righteous behavior. Thus, when we have difficulties in our relationship with God, the problem lies in beliefs and manifests as behaviors. As a result, many of us try and fix our behaviors through willpower without addressing the inaccurate beliefs that are causing them.

THINKING POINT

If our beliefs are so powerful that they are the catalyst to eternity with God (salvation), why is it so difficult for us to believe that our belief of being righteous in Christ makes us righteous, leading to righteous behavior?

APPLICATION

Think of a time in your life when you did something to try and get into good standing with God. Did your act affect your relationship with God or how He related to you? How many 'good works' do you think it takes to get into a righteous standing?

In Romans 3:22 we see that our righteousness is based on our belief in Jesus Christ as the Son of God and our Savior, and not by what we do. Behavior does not make us righteous. If it did, following the Ten Commandments would have justified us and we would not need Jesus or the Cross. Believing we are righteous through the blood of Christ is what is required, and behaviors will naturally follow.

1.3 THE ORIGINATION OF PROBLEMS

Problems (any barrier to God's love) occur when beliefs are not based on the truth and life of the Word of God. Inaccurate beliefs about God's nature and character, therefore how He relates to everyday life, is detrimental to a Christian's relationship with God. This is because inaccurate beliefs are the very basis of spiritual warfare.

> *2 Corinthians 10:4-5 (KJV): (For the weapons of our warfare are not carnal, but mighty through God to the pulling down of strongholds)*
> *(5) Casting down imaginations, and every high thing that exalteth itself against the knowledge of God, and bringing into captivity every thought to the obedience of Christ;*

Let us look at the Greek translation of 2 Corinthians 10:4-5:
"Carnal" is "sarkikos" (σαρκικός): "fleshy or having the nature of flesh".
"Pulling down" is "kathairesis" (καθαίρεσις): "to destroy or destruction".
"Strongholds" is "ochyrōma" (ὀχύρωμα): "arguments and reasoning; or beliefs".
"Imaginations" is "logismos" (λογισμός): "reasoning: such as is hostile to the Christian faith; reckoning; judgement; decision".
Every "high thing" is "hypsōma" (ὕψωμα): "barrier".

In putting this together, 2 Corinthians 10:4-5 is saying that the weapons of our warfare are not of a fleshy nature, or even spiritual for that matter, but mighty through God [for] the destruction of arguments and reasoning, or inaccurate beliefs, because they are a barrier between God and us.

When experiences in life don't line up with what we anticipate, we infer or make up beliefs (inaccurate beliefs) to assimilate experiences with what we already know or believe. Assimilation means fitting new information or experiences in with what we already know in an attempt to make sense of life as a whole.

To make sense of life, we make up inaccurate theology about God when we do not understand how He relates to everyday life.

To make sense of life when it does not, rather than studying God's Word, we make up inaccurate theology about God when we don't understand how He relates to everyday life. This is the barrier (hypsōma) we create between God and ourselves because we cannot worship what we don't know or believe in (John 4:24).

THINKING POINT

Think of a time in your life when you did not understand how God related to a negative experience, such as divorce or losing a child or loved one. How did you justify God's relation to the experience to make sense of life with Him?

The inability to make sense of life with God is the primary motive and source of inaccurate beliefs and false theology that we make up and take as truth, or that we believe as truth just because it is what we have been told. All this happens for the simple reason of trying to justify how God relates to everyday life.

We are logical beings. We need reason and understanding. We take comfort in predictability. We are constantly attempting to make sense of life. We are always comparing new experiences with the experiences of the past to give order and meaning to life (assimilation). We strive to make sense of the world we live in, at the same time as understanding how God relates to everyday life. Sometimes they may not agree with another, thus the feeling that the Christian life is 'not working' or that God is distant.

When we lack understanding, our mind can create new beliefs to make sense of what we do not understand. Knowledge of God's Word will release us from the bondage of trying to make sense of the world when it doesn't.

> *John 8:32 (NIV): Then you will know the truth, and the truth will set you free."*

The world is not able to make sense of itself apart from the Word of God. This is the reason there are so many religions, fads, cults, and new ideologies. People are trying to find meaning and value in this world apart from a relationship with their Creator. And they are left empty.

Beliefs are what we use to achieve meaning and satisfaction in life even if they are not true or lack harmony with the Word of God. This innate need of ours for life to make sense is the primary motive and source of inaccurate beliefs and false theology. We hear or make up inaccurate beliefs that are not consistent with the truth of God's Word, placing our faith in them, when we don't under understand life with God.

These inaccurate beliefs become the motivators of behavior rather than our behavior being motivated by God's truth and perfect love (Hosea 4:6, 1 Corinthians 3:19). The result is problematic behaviors we establish to reinforce inaccurate beliefs to maintain a perverted sense of stability. This is the problem with familiarity. And it's a big problem.

REAL LIFE

While Justin and Renee were serving in junior high youth ministry, they had a student in their life-group who lost her step-mother whom she was close with, only to lose her father three weeks later. How do you make sense of this in understanding how God relates to everyday life?

The answer is, we were not created to experience death. Death is not natural to us. God created us with the intent to live forever in perfect relation with Him (Garden of Eden). Death, regardless of the reason, breaks the bond of love that we were created to have with one another, and it was never meant to be severed. It is never God's desire to take loved ones away from us. The only two people we know of whom God took away were Enoch and Elisha, and they were both taken alive.

God does not need our loved ones in Heaven. He desires them to be here on this earth to be a light unto the world, to save the lost. This is the reason Paul said, although he would prefer going to be with Jesus, it is better for Him to remain in the world (Philippians 1:23-26).

1.4 THE PROBLEM WITH FAMILIARITY

Problematic behaviors (any barriers to experiencing God's perfect love) bring us a false sense of security because they are rooted in familiarity. No matter how destructive a behavior is, there is a sense of perverted comfort with it because it is predictable and familiar. An example would be staying in a dysfunctional relationship, or even emotional eating or turning to 'comfort food', both of which I have struggled with.

> Proverbs 26:11 (NIV): As a dog returns to its vomit, so fools repeat their folly.

There is more comfort in what we know and understand, even when destructive, compared to being confident and secure in God's faithfulness and perfect love. We are creatures of habit. We understand structure; we take comfort in patterns, habits, and predictability even when they are detrimental to us.

Familiarity makes even healthy change difficult. Change without restructuring life Will result in short-lived change because our relationships, behavioral patterns, and

APPLICATION

Think of a time when you developed a bad habit that you knew was unhealthy or destructive, but you still clung to it because it calmed you during stressful times or periods of anxiety.

This is an example of hanging on to familiarity even when it can be destructive.

while change merely deals with the surface. The main difference is summarized as: Our genuine and authentic transformation into our new creation in Christ (2 Corinthians 5:17)!

The purpose of this book is to restructure our life in accordance to the Word of God, giving us the whole picture of living life in the perfect love of Christ. Restructuring our life in God's Word produces intimacy or familiarity with Him, giving us the ability to identify regularities and patterns in our relationship that are producing barriers to experiencing His perfect love. This will be liberating and is what is meant when the Word says that when you know the truth, the truth will set you free (John 8:32).

To see ourselves in the whole picture of God's perfect love, our perception (beliefs) must be established in being *one with Christ*. This can be difficult to believe because we tend to only focus on what we can see, which is our imperfect man (Romans 5:12). Rather than focusing on ourselves or the problems within us, this study will teach us to look solely upon Jesus (Matthew 6:33) and being one with Him (Ephesians 2:15, 1 John 4:17). To fully understand being one with Christ, we must understand what has been

the meaning and value we place on experiences (what we are familiar with) will most likely over-compensate the desired change in behavior we seek.

This book will focus on restructuring our life by laying a solid foundation in the truth and life of God's Word, producing stability in experiencing the perfect love of God in everyday life. Restructuring means something different from change. Restructuring creates a new foundation

REAL LIFE

Before Justin's supernatural transformation, he tried to quit drinking numerous times upon the realization that he was an alcoholic. He tried to change himself. However, Justin continued to frequent the same bars, attend the same parties and bonfires. Everything remained the same except his cognitive decision to quit drinking. Not only were the patterns in his life the same, but so was the dysfunctional concept he held about himself. His feelings of significance remained grounded in his drinking buddies, as well as the flirting and chasing of women that accompanied those environments. Justin's identity and network systems remained the same and he remained unchanged. He had no stability because his desired behavior (not to drink) was not a logical response to the way his life (or system) was constructed. This is the reason the purpose of the Jesus System is to construct a life grounded in the Word of God, where dysfunctional behavior is not logical because it is a life that is fulfilled with God's perfect love.

purchased for us on the Cross: Salvation.

THINKING POINT

Place a pen in a Bible. What will happen to the pen if you were to drop the Bible? What will happen to the pen if you submerged the Bible in water?

Being that we are in Jesus, we are the pen in the Bible. Whatever happens to Jesus (His death and resurrection) has happened to us upon our belief in Him as Lord and Savior. In other words, when God looks at us (the pen), He sees Christ (the Bible) (1 John 4:13, 17; 1 Corinthians 1:30; Ephesians 1:4, 2:15).

1.5 THE DEFINITION OF SALVATION

To understand being one with Christ, we need to understand what Christ accomplished for us through His death and resurrection. When speaking of salvation, most people believe the Gospel only includes being saved from hell or what some call 'fire insurance.' However, there is so much more that we have been given through salvation, specifically, seven inheritances. These are known as the seven definitions of salvation, also known as the complete Gospel or the finished works of Jesus Christ.

To fully understand salvation, we need to look at the original language the Bible was written in, which was Hebrew and Greek. In defining salvation Biblically, when you combine the Greek word for salvation, "sōtēria" (σωτηρία), and the Hebrew word for salvation, 'yĕshuw`ah' (יְשׁוּעָה),

OR

If you combine the Greek word for saved, "sōzō" (σώζω), with the Greek word "sōtēria" (σωτηρία), you will find that both combinations give us the seven definitions of salvation, which are: Saved, healed, delivered (rescued), prospered, protected, preserved, and made whole.

We will look at four verses, for example (see if you can find the others), that all use the same Greek word "sōzō" (σώζω), meaning "to save" or "saved". They are:

1. Mark 5:28 (KJV): For she said, If I may touch but his clothes, I shall be **whole** (sōzō).
2. Luke 8:36 (KJV): They also which saw it told them by what means he that was possessed of the devils was **healed** (sōzō).
3. John 3:17 (KJV): For God sent not his Son into the world to condemn the world; but that the world through him might be **saved** (sōzō).
4. 2 Timothy 4:18 (KJV): And the LORD shall deliver me from every evil work, and will **preserve** (sōzō) me unto his heavenly kingdom.

Salvation means we are saved, healed, delivered, prospered, preserved, protected, and made whole. Just as we are guaranteed of being saved from hell (Romans 5:11, 2 Corinthians 5:21), we have the same guarantee of healing, deliverance, prosperity, protection, preservation, and wholeness.

> **Salvation means we are saved, healed, delivered, prospered, preserved, protected, and made whole.**

The finished works of Christ means that what He accomplished on the Cross, His works or our inheritances of salvation, are finished or already completed in us through our belief in Christ (John 3:16). There is nothing more we can add to Christ's finished works through what we do because Jesus has already finished the work in us (Philippians 2:13). For example, we were made whole when we became saved, therefore life is learning how to live in the wholeness of Christ in that we are one with Him (1 Corinthians 15:10, Ephesians 2:4-6,15-16, Colossians 3:10, Hebrews 13:21).

> *Philippians 2:13 (KJV): For **it is God which worketh in you** both to will and to do of his good pleasure.*

We must grasp this concept of being made whole in Christ, along with the other six inheritances of salvation, to live a life of experiencing God's perfect love. It is because of Christ's love manifesting through salvation that we can have the relationship with God that we were created to experience: A relationship full of life, fulfillment, and wholeness (Psalm 16:11, 2 Peter 1:3).

Contrary to building our life on the foundation of God's Word, it can be easy for us to build our life on what we think is ideal concerning societal standards (social constructions) of how to attain wholeness or fulfillment. Rosenblatt hits on this perfectly:

APPLICATION

God lives in an eternal realm void of time. He lives in the realm of wholeness and completion. Christ's work in you is finished, which is why Paul had confidence in who he was (Philippians 1:6) and why your life as His beloved is not about trying to get wholeness, but learning how to live in the wholeness you already have in Christ.

Instead of viewing yourself as trying to become whole, believe you are already made whole in Christ, and that your life is a journey of learning how to live in His wholeness.

"Indeed, as finite beings, we cannot claim infinite wisdom and our inventions will probably always fall short in comparison to our ideals; we can however, begin to get a closer match between the ideals we pose and the processes we create to attain these ideals" (1994, p.86).

When our ideals for life are in-sync with the ideals that God has for us, specifically, and we rely on Him rather than trying to achieve ideals ourselves, we will obtain a utopian experience (Romans 14:17) because we will experience God's healing, restoration, and rest (Hebrews 4:11). We will experience His perfect love for us.

When we enter His rest, when we become intimate (familiar) with God we will find delight in the LORD (Job 22:21, Isaiah 58:14). And this is what we are going to learn how to do in our journey through this book. We will examine each part of our life, our systems of Belief, Faith, Identity, Communication, and Network, ground them in the truth and life of God's Word, establishing a life fully inter-connected in the Word of God functioning harmoniously as a whole in His perfect love. This journey will continue with our beliefs, and now that we understand the power of beliefs, we need to realize the power of inaccurate beliefs.

THINKING POINT

The only fulfillment in this world is the perfect love of Christ. Contrary to many inaccurate beliefs, God intends for you to enjoy this present, earthly realm. It's not true that the Christian life is not enjoyed because of sin, sickness, strife, deprivation, and sacrifice. God's will for your life is for you to have life and have it more abundantly (John 10:10; Isaiah 58:14)!

Which do you think will provide more fulfillment? The world and what it thinks is fulfilling, or God who is the author of life and the very essence of joy and fulfillment (Psalm 16:11; Ephesians 3:19)?

REAL LIFE

One of the reason beliefs are so powerful, is because what we believe literally changes the structure of your brain. There is an area of the brain that is called the Reticular Activator (RA), located in the Reticular Formation (RF) which is at the base of the brain stem. It is responsible for arousal and motivation, among other functions. The purpose of the RA is to keep our brain on alert, and through being alert, it determines what we subconsciously will notice or ignore. If we did not have this ability through the RF to ignore stimuli, we would continually be in such a sate of distraction that we literally would not be able to function. This is because it is estimated that our brain processes 400 billion bits of information per second (Dispenza, 2007)!

What's interesting, is the structure of the RA literally changes according to what we believe, through a phenomenon known as neural plasticity. Neural plasticity is defined as the ability of a neuron (brain cell) to change their structure, function, and how they are interconnected to other neurons, all in response to stimuli. As the Psychology Dictionary states, neural plasticity can decide whether a neuron will respond to an external stimulus. In other words, neural plasticity determines whether our brain will respond or not to stimuli and is literally determined by what we believe.

This means that our RA chooses to respond according to what we believe. In other words, our brain takes notice to any stimuli that reinforces what we believe, whether negative or positive. For example, if one believes in God's wrath, everything that happens in life that supports this belief will be noticed by the brain, bringing it into consciousness, while any stimuli in opposition to this belief will be ignored. This is the reason those who choose not to believe in God are so blinded by His perfect love and is the reason why the Pharisees could not identify God as a man named Jesus of Nazareth, despite Him performing signs and miracles.

Beliefs are powerful because they shape your brain, thereby shaping our reality, thereby shaping us.

INDIVIDUAL/GROUP DISCUSSION QUESTIONS

1. Why it is so imperative for our beliefs and thoughts to be established in the Word of God? (2 Peter 1:3)

_____
_____
_____
_____

2. In your own words, when do we make up inaccurate beliefs about God? (2 Corinthians 10:4-5; p.6-7)

_____
_____
_____
_____

3. Why is familiarity such a problem? (p.8)

_____
_____
_____
_____

4. In your own words, define the finished works of Christ: (p.10)

_____
_____
_____
_____

5. Why must we understand the seven definitions of salvation or the complete Gospel, to become familiar with God? (John 1:1, 4:24, Romans 1:16; p.11)

    _____

    _____

    _____

    _____

6. Write down one thing you have learned that has meant the most to you:

    _____

    _____

    _____

    _____

CHAPTER 2

THE POWER OF INACCURATE BELIEFS

2.1 INACCURATE BELIEFS

Just as casting a pebble into a pond causes a ripple effect, our beliefs ripple into all areas of life. In fact, beliefs are so powerful that they have eternal ramifications in that they are the catalyst for salvation (John 3:16, Romans 3:22). And just like beliefs are the catalyst for salvation, they are also the catalyst for righteousness, therefore behavior (Romans 3).

THINKING POINT

Your beliefs will either bring you closer to Christ or keep you from experiencing all that He has purchased for your salvation (John 3:16). Nothing is more heartbreaking than a Christian earnestly seeking God with all their heart and might, yet unable to experience His presence because of inaccurate beliefs.

The Bible says we worship God in spirit and truth (John 4:24). All believers have the spirit upon salvation, but how can we worship God if we don't know the truth of who He is? Is it possible to worship what we don't know?

It can be difficult for us to believe that righteousness comes through belief. While we don't experience a problem accepting that belief in Jesus Christ brings us into a relationship with God for eternity, we struggle to accept that beliefs are capable of producing righteousness (Romans 3:22). The result of this disconnect between our head and heart is a striving mentality to earn righteousness through 'works' (Romans 3:20), the very opposite of grace. We believe the lie that our righteousness is based on our 'good works' or what we do rather than God's perfect love and grace. This is how powerful beliefs are in determining your perception of how God sees you, communicates with you, and interacts with you. To grasp the power of beliefs, let us understand what they are, exactly.

Beliefs are personally formed or culturally shared cognitive configurations (thoughts or thought processes) (Wrubel et al., 1981). They are preexisting notions about reality which serve as the perceptual lens that we see and experience life through; to see life through our beliefs determines, in our minds, "how things are" and they shape the understanding of its meaning (Lazarus & Folkman, 1984, p. 63).

THINKING POINT

Are inaccurate beliefs more damaging than sin (Hosea 4:6, James 1:15)? Let us look at it this way: A nonbeliever who has no view of God can be led to repentance and salvation easier than a nonbeliever with inaccurate views of God (1 Timothy 2:4).

Why? Because the inaccurate beliefs, which are often personal and emotionally driven, must be disproven. This can be extremely tough because these beliefs often have decades of reinforcement through experiences that have been perceived inaccurately. A false sense of reality has been created and deeply ingrained into their mentality, into their very being, and has been taking place, in some cases, for a lifetime.

Once inaccurate beliefs are stripped down, eradicated and replaced with the truth of God's Word, an opportunity will be birthed for them to be led to repentance and salvation (Romans 10:17). However, God's presence in an individual's heart can accomplish decades of work in a single moment. These adverse effects of inaccurate beliefs are addressed in Hosea:

Hosea 4:6 (KJV): My people are destroyed for lack of knowledge: because thou hast rejected knowledge.

It is important to note Hosea 4:6 is speaking about believers when it says, "My people," meaning those who believe in God. The lack of knowledge is specifically about the knowledge of God. Secondly, how do we reject the knowledge of God? One way is to fail to read the Word, thus failing to become familiar with God.

The knowledge of God has already been given to us through His Word, therefore it is up to us to read it and to know Him (Ephesians 3:18-19). How well you know Jesus is how well you know the Word, because Jesus was the Word made flesh (John 1:14).

The reason beliefs are powerful is because they determine what fact is, that is, "how things are" in life, shaping the understanding of the reality we live in. They are the thoughts we use to not only make sense of life, but they determine our value and worth, or lack thereof. The reason inaccurate beliefs about God are so powerful is because we will view our false beliefs of God as fact, thus shaping our reality or everyday life *absent* of His true, loving nature and character. We cannot worship what we don't believe in.

Beliefs shape our perception of the god we worship. If our perception of god does not align with the God of the Bible, we will be worshiping nothing but an idol (Ephesians 2:15). When our beliefs are not in harmony with the Word of God, especially concerning the nature and character of God, our false perception of Him will keep us from living life in His perfect love. These inaccurate beliefs are what Paul was talking about in 2 Corinthians:

2 Corinthians 10:5 (KJV): Casting down imaginations, and every high thing that exalteth itself against the knowledge of God, and bringing into captivity every thought to the obedience of Christ.

Our beliefs shape our perception of the god we worship. If our perception of god does not align with the God of the Bible, we will be worshiping nothing but an idol.

If you remember our translation of 2 Corinthians 10:5:
"Imaginations" is "logismos" (λογισμός):
"reasoning, reckoning, computation, and judgment," or thoughts.
Every "high thing" is "hypsōma" (ὕψωμα): "barrier".

And now the translation of Hosea 4:6:
"Lack of knowledge" is "da`ath" (דעת): "perception".

Hosea 4:6 is saying: "My people are destroyed for inaccurate perceptions." These two verses, together, tell us that if our thoughts and perceptions are not accurate and aligned with the Word of God, they will become a barrier between ourselves and experiencing the love that God has intended for us to experience. In other words, inaccurate beliefs are destructive because they will keep us from experiencing grace, the very power of God's Word (Acts 20:24, Romans 1:16).

In fact, we see the value of having knowledge of Christ in 2 Peter1:3:

2 Peter 1:3 (NIV): According to his divine power hath given unto us all things that pertain unto life and godliness, through the knowledge of him [Jesus Christ] that hath called us to glory and virtue.

So, how are inaccurate beliefs created?

The process of creating inaccurate beliefs mirrors the cycle of a lie. First, a little white lie is given. Then we must develop another lie to keep the first one plausible, then another, and another, until the complexity of the lies gets so far-fetched that we lose sight of reality. All for the simple sake of reinforcing our first, white lie. This is the reason there is no such thing as a white lie and why living a life of lies and deceit is torturous and exhausting.

APPLICATION

Think of a time when you told a lie, and then you found yourself creating more lies to reinforce the plausibility of your initial lie.

The cycle of a lie happens with our beliefs as well. We create an inaccurate belief of God and then we must create more false beliefs to keep our first one plausible.

Our beliefs work the same way. Think of a person who experienced the death of a spouse. Their first belief might go something like, "God allowed this to happen, therefore I'll live with it." Then their second spouse leaves them, and they believe God allowed this to happen as well. From this they create another inaccurate belief that God wants them to live alone, thus reinforcing the inaccurate belief that God allowed the previous circumstances to happen. The person then gets lonely and resents God, thinking that He doesn't love them, thus generating another inaccurate belief that they are unlovable. These inaccurate beliefs then create a barrier (hypsōma; Hosea 4:6; 2 Corinthians 10:5) of isolation by habitually sabotaging relationships, even their relationship with God, to keep from being vulnerable as a means of self-preservation, all because it's 'God's will'.

What we fail to understand is that relational 'characteristics', or beliefs that we create from previous relationships, will be projected onto God. We learn how to relate to God through the relationships we have with people. People who are hurt will try to protect themselves by building a wall around their heart that rejects love, even the love of God, as a defense mechanism to keep from being hurt.

When living under inaccurate beliefs of God's nature and character, lies are created and reinforced that becomes a barrier between God and us (Hosea 4:6, 2 Corinthians 10:5). The result will give us the inaccurate perception that life "isn't working" with God because we are unable to freely receive His love and Grace.

> **During these times of feeling distant from God, or that life 'isn't working' with Him, it becomes easy to entertain lies that He does not love us. But keep in mind we are never distant or separated from God, nor does He ever stop loving us.**

During these times of feeling distant from God, or that life 'isn't working' with Him, it becomes easy to entertain lies that He does not love us. But keep in mind we are never distant or separated from God (Romans 8:38-39), nor does He ever stop loving us (James 1:17)! This feeling of distance is not because God stops loving us, but we stop experiencing His presence and love and we stop loving Him.

2.2 WHEN LIFE WITH GOD 'ISN'T WORKING'

The confusion and frustration that accompanies life with God 'not working' is not a new concept. In fact, this same frustration is recorded in the Bible. King Solomon, considered both the richest and wisest man who has ever lived, is the author of Ecclesiastes where he wrote a reflection about life 'not working'.

> *Ecclesiastes 2:10-11 (KJV): And whatsoever mine eyes desired I kept not from them, I withheld not my heart from any joy; for my heart rejoiced in all my labour: and this was my portion of all my labour. (11) Then I looked on all the works that my hands had wrought, and on the labour that I had labored to do: and, behold, all was vanity and vexation of spirit, and there was no profit under the sun.*

In Ecclesiastes 2, King Solomon writes about how he conducted an experiment in search for the meaning of life. He went after anything he wanted for the sake of finding joy and fulfillment. Through his experiment, King Solomon realized that there was no fulfillment in the world despite his vast wealth and endless resources.

> *Ecclesiastes 2:11 (KJV): behold, all was vanity and vexation of spirit, and there was no profit under the sun.*

Vanity is Hebrew for "hebel" (הֶבֶל), and means, "vapor". Vexation is Hebrew for "ra`uwth" (רְעוּת), and means, "striving".

When King Solomon said all was vanity and vexation of spirit, it means there was no fruit from his labor or striving. It produced nothing but a vapor. There was no essence or substance produced from his effort. There was "no profit under the sun".

Life was 'not working' for King Solomon, who had the greatest resources of anyone who has ever lived. In fact, he was so miserable that he ended up hating life (Ecclesiastes 2:17). This same process of trying to find joy and fulfillment in the world happens to many of us. And like King Solomon, when this process fails us it causes us to become frustrated to the point of hating life, or worse, hating God. If we think money and resources can buy us happiness, the richest and wisest man who has ever lived already put that theory to the test, and they failed.

Another example of life 'not working' is in Psalm 73. Asaph writes that when he looked at life, he almost lost his footing:

APPLICATION

Think of a time when you strove to find joy and fulfillment, such as going on a shopping spree or making unreasonable commitments with others for a sense of worth. Or even when you did an act or obligation to try and put yourself in right standing with God.

Burnout and frustration happen because striving produces nothing but a vapor--there is no substance to it. The gratification will only disappear after a while and you will be left striving again with nothing to show for it. This is the reason the only lasting joy and fulfillment in this world, is the presence of God.

Psalm 73:2 (KJV): But as for me, my feet were almost gone; my steps had well nigh slipped. (3) For I was envious at the foolish, when I saw the prosperity of the wicked.

Because of what Asaph thought he was seeing, which was the wicked prospering and the righteous being punished, he developed inaccurate beliefs that were inconsistent with God's nature and character. This is what he meant by his foothold slipping.

This same process of trying to find joy and fulfillment in the world happens to many of us. And like King Solomon, when this process fails us, it causes us to become frustrated to the point of hating life, or worse, hating God.

Ephesians 6:15 speaks of our feet being bound with the gospel of peace. If we are not founded in God's Word, we will eventually slip. This is what was happening to Asaph when he envied the foolish.

Asaph thought he was seeing the wicked prosper while he was being plagued and chastened (punished). This is an example of how what we believe not only changes our perception of reality, but it changes how we interact with God and how we believe He interacts with us. Asaph was noticing what many Christians perceive inaccurately today: What should be happening to the good is happening to the wicked, and what should happen to the wicked is happening to the good. Asaph's inaccurate perception of God was because of inaccurate beliefs.

Let us look at a similar story, the story of Job. Then we will see how King Solomon, Asaph, and Job came to the same revelation of the truth of God's nature and character.

2.3 JOB: WHAT REALLY HAPPENED

Job is the oldest book of the Bible and is where more inaccurate theology comes from than any other book. The most widely accepted incorrect belief of God, coming from the book of Job, is that God made an agreement with Satan that turned Job over to Satan.

Our belief in God placing Job in the hands of Satan or not, will determine our belief in the very nature of God Himself. It will either create detrimental inaccurate beliefs about the character of God, or will show us His loving nature.

APPLICATION

Can you remember a time when you thought God 'handed' you over to Satan; when something went very wrong in your life and you thought God orchestrated it? How would it change your view of God if you realized that it was not only His desire to keep this from happening to you, but He also desired to protect you from it? Just because God 'allowed' it doesn't mean He orchestrated it. It goes back to His perfect gift to us of free will.

> *Job 1:8 (KJV): And the LORD said to Satan, hast thou considered my servant Job, that there is none like him in the earth, a perfect and upright man, one that feareth God, and escheweth evil?*

We can understand where the misunderstanding comes from when people read Job 1:8. "Have you considered my servant Job?" does indeed sound like God is offering Job to Satan. However, in Hebrew, the accurate translation of what God is saying to Satan is, "Have you set your heart against Job?"

> *Job 1:8 (YLT): And Jehovah saith unto the Adversary, `Hast thou set thy heart against My servant, Job, because there is none like him in the land, a man perfect and upright, fearing God, and turning aside from evil?'*

Just reflect for a moment on how this difference in translations affects our perception of God. Think of how it portrays polar-opposites of His nature and character. One exemplifies God as a god who offers His beloved child to evil saying, "Here, do what you want to him. I bet he won't curse me!" The other simply acknowledged Satan having his heart set on attacking Job.

The truth is, God acknowledged that Satan already had his mind made up on attacking Job, just like he attacks many of us. And what most people fail to recognize is that after God acknowledged Satan's desire to attack Job, God defended Job in the same breath! God did this because He already knew Satan's intent, otherwise, why would He stick up for Job?

THINKING POINT

Rather than handing Job over to Satan, God stuck up for Job and was his advocate, just like it states in 1 John:

> 1 John 2:1 (KJV): My dear children, I write this to you so that you will not sin. But if anybody does sin, we have an advocate with the Father – Jesus Christ, the Righteous one.

Next time you experience a negative or traumatic event in your life and are tempted to blame God like Job did, remember that God is sticking up for you. He is your advocate and it is His desire to protect you and to keep you from harm (Psalm 18:2, 61:3, Jeremiah 29:33).

The next verse that gives us inaccurate beliefs is Job 1:12:

> Job 1:12 (KJV): And the LORD said unto Satan, Behold, all that he hath is in thy power; only upon himself put not forth thine hand. So Satan went forth from the presence of the LORD.

The word "behold" gives people the perception that this was the point in time when God handed Job over. However, the way "behold" is used in the Bible is to explain an object or act that has *already* taken place. Let us look at a few examples:

> Genesis 1:29 (KJV): And God said, Behold, I **have given** you every herb bearing seed, which is upon the face of all the earth, and every tree, in which is the fruit of a tree yielding seed; to you it shall be for meat.

Genesis 1:29 makes it clear that "behold" is expressing something that already happened, because following it are the words "have given" and "which is upon", which are both past tense. Another example is in Luke 2:

> Luke 2:10-11 (KJV): And the angel said to them, Fear not: for, behold, I bring you good tidings of great joy, which shall be to all people. (11) For unto you **is born this day** in the city of David a Savior, which is Christ the LORD.

It is clear in Luke 2:10 when the angel used the word "behold," he was informing them of Christ's birth in the past tense, meaning it had already happened.

It is important to understand that the very act of God placing Job in the hands of Satan, as a result of Satan coming to tempt God with a challenge, is in direct contradiction to James 1.

> James 1:13 (KJV): Let no man say when he is tempted, I am tempted of God: for God cannot be tempted with evil, neither tempteth he any man:

The belief that Job was not in the hands of Satan would mean that we believe

Satan came to God with the premeditation of tempting Him through a challenge that would result in the fate of Job's life. James shows us that God cannot be tempted by evil, let alone by the devil in using humans as subjects. It shows us that God didn't tempt Job by causing him hardship to see if he would remain righteous.

In Jeremiah 29 we see not only God's intent for our lives, but also that He will not bring harm unto us:

> Jeremiah 29:11 (NIV): For I know the plans I have for you," declares the LORD, "plans to prosper you and **not to harm you**, plans to give you hope and a future.

Harm is emotional, mental, and/or physical. God would never put us, or Job, in the way of harm in an emotional, mental, and/or physical context. It is not His plan.

The Hebrew word for "harm" is "ra`" (רַע), and means, "bad, malignant, unpleasant, displeasing, worse than, sad, unhappy, hurtful, wicked, misery, calamity, distress, adversity, injury, wrong, etc.".

What is interesting is that it comes from the root word "ra`a`" (רָעַע), which means, "evil". Evil is the absence of God. God will never tempt us with evil or the absence of Himself, or by causing sadness, misery, injury, hurt, or to cause bad, malignant, unpleasant, displeasing, worse than, unhappy, wicked, calamity, distress, adversity, or wrong.

What happened to Job was not the result of a bet between God and Satan, nor was Job being placed in the hands of Satan a result either. Job placed himself in the hands of Satan. Despite Job living a righteous life, he lived in fear because of his inaccurate beliefs.

THINKING POINT

Why do we think God needs to use "evil" to teach us lessons or to grow and mature us? Do we believe the God of all wisdom and knowledge, our loving Creator, lacks the ability to teach us without harming us or bringing evil upon us?

Even while having a righteous heart, all it takes to give the enemy a foothold in our life is an inaccurate belief about God, or fear.

Job 3:25 (KJV): For the thing which I greatly feared is come upon me, and that which I was afraid of is come unto me.

Job was credited as being righteous because of the condition of his heart. The problem was with his inaccurate beliefs, which enabled him to live in fear because of a lack of knowledge of God. This lack of knowledge produced a barrier to living in God's protection (2 Corinthians 10:5).

Even while having a righteous heart, all it takes to give the enemy a foothold in our life is an inaccurate belief about God, or fear. Worry, stress, and anxiety are all symptoms of an unbelieving heart, rooted in unbelief that God will not do what He promised in His Word. Fear paralyzes our mind, keeping us from making decisions influenced by the Holy Spirit while being saturated in the peace and love of God's presence.

To understand what Job feared, we will go back to Chapter 1:

> *Job 1:5 (KJV): And it was so, when the days of their feasting were gone about, that Job sent and sanctified them, and rose up early in the morning, and offered burnt offerings according to the number of them all: for Job said, It may be that my sons have sinned, and cursed God in their hearts. Thus did Job continually.*

Job lived in fear of his children sinning. He would get up every morning and offer burnt offerings on their behalf. This was Job's social construction--his inaccurate belief. This would be the same today as a parent praying to God every morning asking forgiveness for any sins their children may have committed.

THINKING POINT

God has given us dominion over the earth (Genesis 1:26) and He has stripped the enemy of all power and authority (Colossians 2:15). This means that the only authority the enemy has in our lives, is the authority we give him. This happens when we live in fear; when we do not believe God will do what His Word promises us, or when we believe something about ourselves that is not in accordance with His Word. We make decision in fear, rather than in the peace and stability of God's presence and perfect love.

Is there something that you believe about you or your life that when you compare it to God's Word, you know it is a lie?

Anytime we give into or dwell on fear, we are giving more authority to the kingdom of darkness than to the power of God. Because Job lived in fear, he put himself into the hands of Satan and gave him the authority to take control of his life. Job failed to realize this, so who do you think he blamed? Just like many of us, Job blamed God.

> **Anytime we give into or dwell on fear, we are giving more authority to the kingdom of darkness than to the power of God.**

> *Job 1:21 (KJV): And said, naked came I out of my mother's womb, and naked I shall return thither: the LORD gave, and **the LORD hath taken away;** blessed be the name of the LORD.*

Half of Job's theology is right in that he believes the LORD gives because every good thing comes from the LORD (James 1:17). The other half of his theology, that the LORD takes away, is deathly inaccurate. Job's way of understanding what was happening in his life was to believe that God is a God who takes away.

Job blamed God, just like we're tempted to do when life does not make sense or is simply 'not working'. It's logical to understand that inflicting natural disasters, or sickness and diseases, upon us or causing a loved one or child to die does not constitute bringing an 'abundance of life' upon us.

THINKING POINT

This theology of the "LORD taking away" does not fit into the life of Jesus, who is the Word made flesh (John 1:1, 14). Can you think of one time in the Bible where Jesus took something away from someone? In fact, can you think of one time where Jesus left an individual worse off than when He found them? This theology of the Lord 'taking away' is not consistent with His love and nature.

However, if we use logic and reason, and more importantly scripture, 'taking away' is characteristic of the thief that comes to steal, kill, and destroy.

> *John 10:10 (NKJV): The thief does not come except to steal, and to kill, and to destroy. I have come that they may have life, and that they may have it more abundantly.*

There is one thing that fear does very well, and it is making us think illogically and without reason. This is why when we make decisions based on fear, we can look back and think to ourselves, "What was I thinking!"

In Job 38, God responds to Job's inaccurate belief that He "takes away":

APPLICATION

Can you remember a decision you made that was based on fear, and after the decision you regretted it? Fear paralyzes our prefrontal cortex, the part of our brain where we use logic and reason, or think. When we dwell on fear we don't make logical decisions, and the decisions we make we are most likely to regret. This is the reason it is imperative to make decisions based in the peace and love of God's presence.

> *Job 38:2-3 (KJV): Who is this that darkeneth counsel by words without knowledge? (3) Gird up now thy loins like a man; for I will demand of thee, and answer thou me.*

God told Job he didn't know what he was talking about and instructed him to prepare himself like a man because correction was coming. God put Job in his place by asking Him questions that exposed his desperate attempt to create inaccurate theology about God to make sense of his life 'not working.' God addressed Job's inaccurate theology directly in Job 40:

> Job 40:8 (KJV): Wilt thou disannul my judgment? Wilt thou condemn me, that thou mayest be righteous?

Judgment can be good or bad. God can judge for us or against us. Upon our salvation, God's judgment is always good and favorable towards us because Christ took on our 'bad' judgment. He is our advocate (1 John 2:1-2). God voiced His good and favorable judgment of Job when He defended him after Satan had set his heart on him. Just like Job, we disannul God's good and favorable judgment when we blame Him for life 'not working'.

> **Upon our salvation, God's judgment for us is always good and favorable because Christ took on our 'bad' judgment.**

If Job would have prayed as soon as he heard the first report, God would have answered, Job would have repented, and God would have protected and restored Him. When Job repented, God revealed Himself to Job and his knowledge of God became accurate. Job finally saw God as opposed to merely hearing of Him.

> Job 42:5-6 (KJV): I have heard of thee by the hearing of the ear: but now mine eye seeth thee. (6) Wherefore I abhor myself, and repent in dust and ashes.

REAL LIFE

If you remember back when hurricane Katrina hit Louisiana, there was a common belief that God was bringing judgment to the city of New Orleans.

If that were the case, why do we send aide to the victims of hurricanes, tsunamis, and earthquakes if we believe God is teaching them a lesson? Would we not be acting in opposition to God's will?

This logic that God sends natural disasters, sickness, and death to teach us lessons, such as in Job, is illogical and the polar opposite of God's nature and character (Isaiah 54:9-10).

2.4 THE CONCLUSION OF JOB, KING SOLOMON, AND ASAPH

King Solomon and Asaph came to the same conclusion that Job came to once they received a true and accurate revelation of God, enabling them to see and experience Him intimately. They had their inaccurate beliefs and false perceptions eradicated by the revelation of God's goodness and His perfect love for them.

King Solomon's conclusion:

> Ecclesiastes 2:24-26 (KJV): There is nothing better for a man, than that he

should eat and drink, and that he should make his soul enjoy good in his labor. This also I saw, that it was from the hand of God. (25) For who can eat, or who else can hasten hereunto, more than I? (26) For God giveth to a man that is good in His sight wisdom, and knowledge, and joy...

Asaph's conclusion:

Psalm 73:16-17 (KJV): When I thought to know this, it was too painful for me; (17) Until I went into the sanctuary of God; then understood I their end.

Sometimes the revelations that change our perspective aren't necessarily revealing the goodness of God, but rather His knowledge and spiritual wisdom that enables us to see the reality of this world apart from the truth and life of His Word. We see the success of others, yet we see how truly empty and lonely they are because they do not know the love they have been created to know: The perfect love of God.

> **The greatest thing Satan can steal from our hearts is the truth of God's perfect love, the truth of His Grace, the truth of His nature and the truth of His character.**

John 10:10 (KJV): The thief cometh not, but for to steal, and to kill, and to destroy: I am come that they might have life, and that they might have it more abundantly.

The greatest thing Satan can steal from our hearts is the truth of God's perfect love (2 Peter 1:3), the truth of His Grace, the truth of His nature and the truth of His character. When the enemy steals the truth of God's Word from our hearts, we believe his lies and exalt inaccurate beliefs above the Word of God, allowing them to become a barrier to living in God's rest, or His perfect love (2 Corinthians 10:5).

> **When the enemy steals the truth of God's Word, we believe his lies and exalt inaccurate beliefs above the Word of God, allowing them to become a barrier to living in God's rest or His perfect love.**

God's perfect love is the revelation that came to King Solomon, Asaph, and Job. Knowing the true nature of God changed their perception of reality as it will do for us (2 Peter 1:3). They saw the whole picture of God's perfect love for them.

When we lack the revelation of God's love, like King Solomon, Asaph, and Job, how do we seek it for ourselves?

*Ephesians 3:9 (KJV): And to make all men see what is the **fellowship** of the mystery, which from the beginning of the world hath been hid in God, who created all things by Jesus Christ:*

First, we need to understand what the mystery is?

*Ephesians 6:19 (KJV): And for me, that utterance may be given unto me, that I may open my mouth boldly, to make known the **mystery of the gospel**.*

The mystery pertains to the gospel or the good news. We find out more, specifically, in Colossians:

> *Colossians 1:26 (KJV): Even the mystery which hath been hid from ages and from generations, but now is* **made manifest** *to his saints:*

What has been made manifest?

> *Colossians 1:27 (KJV): To whom God would make known what is the riches of the glory of this mystery among the Gentiles; which is* **Christ in you**, *the hope of glory:*

In these verses are the keywords: fellowship, gospel, made manifest, and Christ in you. What or who do these keywords sound characteristic of? Here is a hint, who:

1. Is one-third of the Trinity?
2. Enables fellowship with God within us?
3. Enables God's love to manifest through us into the world?
4. Manifests as Christ being in us?

> *Ephesians 2:15 (NIV): by setting aside in his flesh the law with its commands and regulations. His purpose was to create in himself one new humanity out of the two, thus making peace;*

How did God create in Himself one new humanity out of two? By giving us the *Holy Spirit*, and it is through the Holy Spirit, the "mystery," that we have access to the revelations of the Gospel of Jesus Christ because we are one with Him!

The keywords of fellowship, gospel, manifest, and Christ in you are all characteristics of the Holy Spirit, specifically, living a Holy Spirit-filled life.

> *Ephesians 1:17 (KJV): That the God of our LORD Jesus Christ, the Father of glory, may give unto you the spirit of wisdom and revelation in the knowledge of him:*

In Ephesians 1:17, we see that it is through the Holy Spirit, also known as the spirit of wisdom and revelation, that we have knowledge and understanding of the mysteries of God The mystery is the revelation or the knowledge of His gospel of *Grace*.

There is no greater way to know more of God than through reading His Word and being continuously filled with His Spirit.

There is no greater way to know more of God than through reading His Word and being continuously filled with His Spirit. In God's Word and through His Spirit are where revelations come, where guidance comes, as well as direction, purpose, fulfillment, joy, peace, and the fullness of God. It is the place where the intimate revelations of His love for us takes place. This place is God's rest—it is His presence.

These revelations we have through the Word and the Holy Spirit are what opens our eyes and changes our perception of reality, as it did for King Solomon, Asaph, and Job. It is through the truth of God's Word and the Holy Spirit, that is already within us, where inaccurate beliefs are eradicated and replaced with the truth and life of God's perfect love. It is through the Gospel that we understand reality is not what the world sees or understands or teaches us, but reality is the truth and life of God's perfect love that He freely gives us. It is what we have been created to live in, in God's rest, and what the world so desperately craves.

INDIVIDUAL/GROUP DISCUSSION QUESTIONS

1. Why are inaccurate beliefs about God so destructive? (Hosea 4:6; 2 Corinthians 10:5; p.17)

_____
_____
_____
_____

2. When life seems to be 'not working', why is it important to align our perception of life to the Word of God? (Psalm 16:11, Proverbs 3:5)

_____
_____
_____
_____

3. What is the definition of evil? (p.22)

_____
_____
_____
_____

4. How did Job place himself in the hands of Satan (p.22-23)

_____
_____
_____
_____

5. Why do we know that the only authority the enemy has, is the authority that we give him? (Genesis 1:26, Colossians 2:15; p.23 Thinking Point)

_____
_____
_____
_____

6. Why is it so crucial to understand that rather than God handing Job over to Satan, Job placed himself into Satan's hands through living in fear? (John 10:10)

_____

_____

_____

_____

7. What is the best way to continue learning about our LORD Jesus Christ? (Ephesians 1:17; p.27)

_____

_____

_____

_____

CHAPTER 3

BELIEFS OF TRUTH

3.1 THE SOVEREIGNTY OF GOD

Now that we understand the power of beliefs, as well as inaccurate beliefs, we will address some common inaccurate beliefs about God and replace them with the truth of His Word. When we study the Word of God, as well as in our study of how God relates to everyday life, there are Biblical principles that we must understand to establish accurate beliefs in God's nature and character. Founding these principles of God's sovereignty, the law of goodness, God's wrath and judgment, and super-abounding grace in the truth of God's Word will help us better understand scriptures, like in the Book of Job for example. They will also be crucial for us to understand the whole picture of living everyday life in God's perfect love.

The first principle we will discuss is the sovereignty of God.

> *Daniel 4:6 (NIV): Seven times will pass by for you until you acknowledge that the Most High is sovereign over the kingdom of men and gives them to anyone He wishes.*

Some translations, such as the KJV, use the term "LORD God" instead of "sovereign," which are synonymous. Sovereign means "one who exercises supreme authority within a limited sphere" (Merriam-Webster).

Because God is sovereign, He can do whatever He desires, but He is limited to His Word or His "sphere" because it is who He is, His nature and character, the way, the truth, and the life (John 14:6).

The doctrine that God can do whatever, whenever He wants is a paradox, meaning it is true and not true. God does have supreme authority, and because He has supreme authority, He has the power to establish rules or laws. But because He is sovereign, He abides by His rules and laws.

God can do whatever He desires, but is limited to His Word or His "sphere" because it is who He is, His Word, His nature and character, the way, the truth, and the life (John 14:6).

If God went against His rules, or Word, He would be a God that is characterized as a dictator, a tyrannical ruler, a hypocrite and, ultimately, a sinner through disobedience to His own being. God is the Word and the Word is God (John 1:1). God can't go against Himself. And we know God will never deviate from His Word or who He is because He does not change like shifting shadows.

> *James 1:17 (NIV): Every good and perfect gift is from above, coming down from the Father of the heavenly lights, who does not change like shifting shadows.*

THINKING POINT

Religion has perverted the definition of sovereignty by teaching us that God can do whatever, whenever He wants. Why? I believe it is because it is easier to blame God for experiences we do not understand rather than taking responsibility for ourselves. I also believe it is because it is difficult to acknowledge that we live in a fallen world and experience the sin and its consequences of others.

If God has all power and authority, why doesn't He strike down evil people such as Adolf Hitler or Anton LaVey (the author of the Satanic bible)? Let us see why:

In Genesis 1:28, we see one of God's first rules, or laws, in that He gave humankind control over the earth. God is a Spirit (John 4:24) and lives in the spiritual realm. We are physical, and God has given us control over the physical realm. Therefore, God can never force His Will upon us. He needs our permission to act through us and is why He placed His Spirit within us upon our consent (salvation), that we may choose through free will to do His Will: To love as Christ.

This is the perfect love of God--giving His creation the pure essence of free will. Being that we have free will, we can choose to have relation with God or not to. When we chose not to be with God, by default, we choose evil because evil is the absence of God, specifically, the absence of a loving God (1 John 4:8). This is the reason God could not tempt Job, or us, with evil because God cannot tempt us with the absence of Himself (Hebrews 13:5).

When we experience evil in this world it is because people, through their ability to exercise their free will, have made decisions absent of God's love.

When we are irresponsible with what God has entrusted to us, when we do not love as God loves, we will feel the consequences as a person, as a family, as a society, and as humankind.

Free will is the reason we can experience the consequences of the sin of others, such as drunk drivers, starving children due to corporate greed, divorce, etc. When we are irresponsible with what God has entrusted to us, when we do not love as God loves, we will feel the consequences as a person, as a family, as a society, as humankind. This is the root of why bad things happen to good people. Free will gives individuals the ability to choose selfishness over love. Not only do we feel the consequences, but so does God:

> Hebrews 4:14-15 (KJV): Seeing then that we have a great high priest, that is passed into the heavens, Jesus the Son of God, let us hold fast our profession. (15) For we have not a high priest which cannot be touched with the feeling of our infirmities;

When we experience hurts and pains, it is easy for us to believe that God is oblivious to how we feel. The truth is, He feels our hurts and pains as much as we do. God identifies with what we go through and what we feel. He is right there along with us. The Greek word for infirmities in Hebrews 4:15 is "astheneia" (ἀσθένεια), and means, "the native weakness, frailty, feebleness of health or sickness, of the body". Whatever we are feeling, good or bad, God is feeling it right there with us because He is touched by what we feel!

When speaking of sovereignty, I saw this article a day or two after the California mass shootings in December of 2015. And for once, I agreed. God isn't fixing our hate problems and violence, nor will He.

Why?

Because we are the answer. God has empowered us to change the world (Acts 1:8). The Holy Spirit has given us everything we need, which is inside of us, to bring God's perfect love into the world. We do not need more laws to govern how we live; we need hearts to change becoming whole in the perfect love of Christ.

The only way this world will change is when God's love manifests through us into it. Often, we are the answer to our own prayers because of who we are in Christ. In this world we are like Christ (1 John 4:17), and together we are the body of Christ.

Considering what we have just learned about the sovereignty of God, how would you explain Daniel 4:6?

Daniel 4:6 (NIV): Seven times will pass by for you until you acknowledge that the Most High is sovereign over the kingdom of men and gives them to anyone He wishes.

APPLICATION

When was the last time you made a decision not to love someone? Did you realize that you were making a decision void of God's love? Being that God is love (John 4:8), when we make decisions absent of love, we are making decisions absent of God.

If God is sovereign, which means He makes rules or laws and abides by them, and He has given dominion over the earth to man, how can He give the kingdoms of man to anyone He wishes?

Being that God has given dominion of the earth to man, He essentially has given the kingdoms of man to anyone He wishes, in that He has allowed humankind to choose for themselves (free will) who will govern them. This happens in democratic elections, or in the ability of a person through their free will to take over a state or nation by force, such as in a dictatorship, for example.

God's sovereignty, Him having all authority and giving all authority to man, is an example of a paradox, which is two opposing realities that are both true.

Biblical examples of a paradox are that to live, we must die (Galatians 2:20, Mark 8:35), and that the last shall be first and the first last (Matthew 19:30, 20:16). God is a God of paradoxes and He does them very well. He has supreme control over everything, yet at the same time He has given humankind the most precious gift of love: Free will.

Because of God's sovereignty and perfect love, He has given us both free will and dominion over the earth. God cannot force His will or desire upon us, which is to help and direct us unless we give Him permission (Matthew 6:33). God's will and desire is to help us in every facet of life (Proverbs 16:9) and we see this in our next principle of discussion: The law of goodness.

3.2 THE LAW OF GOODNESS

The second principle we will discuss to establish beliefs of truth in God's nature and character is the goodness of God. When we talked about Job, we concluded that the belief Job had about God being responsible for the destruction of his health and family was inaccurate. Now we will understand why it is inaccurate: That it is the goodness of God that brings people to Him (Romans 2:4).

Throughout the book of Leviticus there is an ongoing Biblical principle that if we can help someone in need and we do not, we are guilty of sin. In other words, for example, if we see someone about to be murdered and we can stop it, but we do not, we are guilty of murder. This is also shown in James 4:

> James 4:17 (KJV):
> Therefore to him that knoweth to do good, and doeth it not, to him it is sin.

APPLICATION

Have you ever thought that winning the lottery would solve all your problems? I have. Most believe that winning the lottery will help relieve financial woes. However, research shows that most people who win the lottery end up filing bankruptcy within years of winning. They end up worse off than before. This stat has been used to argue against social welfare programs. God is perfect in all His ways. He will never give us help that will end up harming us or leaving us worse off than before He helped.

We always need to make sure our heart's desires are aligned to His and that just because we may not be perceiving His help in the present, it does not mean that He is not helping. He is just at work behind the scenes allowing us to grow and mature into what He is preparing us for.

This principle of Leviticus and James 4:17 is the Word of God; it is truth. God and the Word are synonymous--they are one (John 1:1). When the Bible tells us to do something, it is because it is the nature of God, who He is, and His heart's desire.

In James 4:17, we see that goodness is based on *knowledge and ability*. We need both the knowledge and the ability, to actually *do* good. Missing just one of these will make one incapable of doing good. God will help us in every aspect of life, not only because He has the knowledge and ability, but because it is His desire, His perfect, loving nature; it is who He is. Because it says this in His Word, and we know His Word is the very essence of His being, we know this is true. God is sovereign. He is the Word and the Word is Him.

If God turned His back on Job and sent Him into the hands of Satan knowing the outcome, God would have sinned because He had the knowledge and ability to protect and help Job. What most people do not understand is that it is His desire, His very nature, to help and guide us in every step of life (Proverbs 16:9, 20:24, James 1:5, John 14:16, Matthew 11:28).

> *Jeremiah 29:13 (NIV): You will seek me and find me when you seek me with all your heart.*

However, God cannot help those who will not allow Him to help or who are trying to help themselves. God was unable to help Job until Job sought Him and asked for help. God chooses to set aside His all-knowing power, authority, and ability because of His perfect gift of free will. This is one of the reasons why Jesus Christ had to come in the flesh, because God could not force His will on humankind for the very reason of giving humankind free will and dominion over the earth.

The law of goodness does not mean the help God gives us will always be what we think, but what is best for us to grow and mature to fulfill what He has purposed for us. Regardless, we must always remember it is His nature and perfect love to give us help and direction in every area of our life (Proverbs 2:1-12, 3:5-6, 21-23, 5:21, 16:9, Matthew 11:28, John 14:16, James 1:5, Ephesians 3:20). But we must trust Him and seek Him first (Jeremiah 29:13, Matthew 6:33).

> *Psalm 37:23 (NLT): The LORD directs the steps of the godly. He delights in **every detail** of their lives.*

> *Proverbs 16:9 (KJV): A man's heart deviseth his way: but the LORD directeth his **steps.***

THINKING POINT

How do we know where God is directing our steps if our focus is not consistently on Him?

How many circumstances have we reluctantly been through that could have been avoided if we were focused on God's presence--our path of life (Psalm 16:11)? Instead, it is easy for us to try and carry our own cares or even the cares of others, leading to stress, anxiety, and fear and, therefore, bad decisions (1 Peter 5:7)

3.3 GOD'S WRATH AND JUDGMENT

Now that we have discussed some of the positive characteristics of God, it is vital to establish accurate beliefs of His wrath and judgment towards man. Inaccurate beliefs of God's wrath and judgment are the most detrimental perceptions a believer can have about God because they can be polar-opposite of His nature and what Christ accomplished on the Cross. Viewing God through a paradigm outside of righteousness by faith through Grace will only produce fear.

> Inaccurate beliefs of God's wrath and judgment are the most detrimental perceptions a believer can have about God because they can be polar-opposite of His nature and what Christ accomplished on the Cross.

Inaccurate beliefs of the wrath and judgment of God hardwires a "works mentality" that is relentless and cannot be appeased, leading to condemnation and guilt. A false belief in an angry God sending down His wrath and judgment gives birth to a vicious cycle of trying to satisfy the innate fear that 'I am not right', 'I am not good enough', or 'I must do more'. Living under inaccurate beliefs of God's wrath and judgment leads to a lifestyle of trying to obtain righteousness or striving to get into God's favor through 'works'. This is living under that law and it will fail you.

> To really understand what Christ accomplished on the Cross, we need to understand the wrath of God was appeased when Jesus Christ took the judgment of the world upon Himself, paying for every sin past, present, and future.

To believe that our 'works', or what we do, can add life to the finished works of Jesus (salvation) is a lie. This lie will only lead to more failure, perpetuating increased amounts of stress and fear, all while driving us to greater lengths to perform and appease the wrath and judgment we believe we deserve or that we believe God is sending upon us.

This cycle will continue until it inevitably leads to burnout or even worse, we become so bitter and hurt from life 'not working' with God that we turn our back on Him. In doing so, we close the door of our heart from receiving the only and permanent answer: His unconditional love and perfect gift of Grace.

To really understand what Christ accomplished on the Cross, we need to understand the wrath of God was appeased when Jesus Christ took the judgment of the world upon himself, paying for every sin past, present, and future.

Let's look at this in scripture:

> *1 John 2:2 (KJV): And He [Jesus] is the **propitiation** of our sins: and not for ours only, but also for the sins of the whole world.*

The Greek word for "propitiation" is "hilasmos" (ἱλασμός), and means, "atoning sacrifice". When Jesus Christ died on the Cross, He experienced what was supposed to be our judgment when He exchanged His righteousness for our *our sins* (2 Corinthians 5:21). Because Christ paid for our sins, people do not go to hell because of their sins, they go to hell because they reject the propitiation of Jesus

> **Because Christ paid for the sins of the world, people do not go to hell because of their sins, they go to hell because they reject the propitiation of Jesus Christ for their sins.**

It is important to note in John 12:32, the word "men" is italicized in most Bibles, meaning it is not in the original manuscripts. We know the word of God is inerrant, meaning it is free from error, untruths, or contradictions. So, when the Word seems to contradict itself, we know it is from our lack of understanding or from an error made in translation from its original language.

The phrase "will draw all men unto me" is speaking of when Jesus was raised on the Cross, that it would draw all men unto Him. Men being drawn to Jesus being raised on the Cross seems to be a contradiction to 1 Corinthians 1:23, that says the Cross is a stumbling block to the Jews and foolishness to the Gentiles. Through this we know that Christ being raised on the Cross did not draw all men unto Him.

Christ for their sins.

*John 12:31-32 (KJV): Now is the judgment of this world: now shall the prince of this world be cast out. (32) And I, if I be lifted up from the earth, will draw all **men** unto me.*

APPLICATION

Think back to a time when you thought God was sending His wrath upon you or punishing you.

It is important to differentiate when we experience the natural consequences of our sin and the wrath and judgment of God. We as children of Grace will never experience the wrath and judgement of God because Christ took it for us. This is the reason we have peace with God (Romans 5:1). However, we are not immune to sin's natural consequences.

When we take the context of John 12 into consideration, which is the judgment of the world, what John 12:32 is saying is that when Christ was raised on the Cross, all *judgment* (not men) came unto Him. This is the accurate translation of John 12:32. I believe the translators' train of thought was that when humankind realizes that Christ took the judgment of the world on the Cross, this knowledge or revelation of Grace would draw "all men" unto Him, because the Cross is the purest essence of God's perfect love and Grace. Unfortunately, this is not what the translation communicates, confusing readers.

When Christ was raised on the cross, we know the judgment of the entire world happened "now", or at that moment in time. Christ appeased the judgment of God for the entire world that we might live in peace with Him. Our God is a God of peace (Romans 5:1, 15:33, 16:20, 2 Corinthians 13:11, Philippians 4:9, 1 Thessalonians 5:23, Hebrews 13:20).

Now, I am not saying that judgment will not occur, because it will when Christ returns (2 Corinthians 5:10). What I am saying is until the day of Christ's return, judgment day, God has established a covenant of peace with man so that His wrath and judgment will not take place until then. This is because God's judgment has been appeased in the body of Christ. In other words, we as children of Grace are preserved perfect, spotless, and blameless (1 Thessalonians 5:23; Jude 1:1).

God's Word clearly states that a child of Grace will not come unto judgment (John 3:18, 5:24, 6:37, Romans 5:1, 8:1, 1 Corinthians 11:32).

On judgment day there will be two judgments:

1. The Judgment Seat of Christ (1 Peter 1:7, 1 Corinthians 3:13) where the works, words, thoughts, etc., of believers, will be tested by fire.
2. The Great White Throne Judgment (Jude 1:6-7, 2 Peter 2:4) where the judgment of the wicked or those who rejected Jesus Christ as Savior, as well as the fallen angels, will take place.

We are saved from God's wrath (Romans 5:9) because Christ took our judgement (John 12:32), appeasing the price for all sin, past, present, and future (Colossians 2:13).

> Romans 5:9 (KJV): Much more then, being now justified by his blood, we shall be saved from wrath through him.

THINKING POINT

If Jesus took our 'bad' judgment on the cross (John 12:32), what other judgment is left other than favorable?

Now, let us better understand what will take place on judgment day. The name "Judgment Seat of Christ" that is used in many translations does not give the accurate portrayal of what really happens at the Judgment Seat of Christ. The Greek Word for "Judgment Seat" is "bēma" (βῆμα), accurately translated as the Bema Seat of Christ. The Bema seat is reference to a structure built by Herod resembling a throne at Caesarea from which he viewed games and made speeches. It is from this structure that the Grecian victor of the games received their reward, which was a wreath crown of leaves.

The Judgement Seat of Christ is where believers will have a favorable judgment on their actions during this life, thus receiving their rewards or crowns, or possibly losing them.

The Judgment Seat of Christ is where believers will have a favorable judgment on their actions during this life, thus receiving their rewards or crowns, or possibly losing them (1 Corinthians 3:14, 2 Corinthians 5:9-10, 1 John 2:28, 1 Thessalonians 2:19-20, 1 Timothy 6:18-19).

The Bible promises us confidence on judgment day (1 John 4:17-18). When our works are tested by fire, being that we are covered by the blood of Christ, any works that are inconsistent with the Word of God will be consumed by the fire, purifying us (Hebrews 3:1). God lives in eternity in the spiritual realm, not governed by time, seeing us in our eternal state purified by the blood of Christ. The purifying nature of Christ's blood is why God sees us, today, perfect and blameless (Colossians 1:22).

When speaking of God's wrath and judgment, God established a covenant of peace through reconciliation with man (Ephesians 2:16, Colossians 1:20, Romans 5:10) because it is the goodness of God that draws man to Him (Romans 2:4).

Now we will address a few verses that bring confusion about God's judgment.

Matthew 7:1 (KJV): Judge not, that ye be not judged.

People read this verse and stop reading further, attributing this verse to God judging those who judge others. If we read the next verse, we will understand its context.

Matthew 7:2 (KJV): For with what judgment ye judge, ye shall be judged: and with what measure ye mete, it shall be measured to you again.

When we judge others, we will not only believe others are judging us with the same measure we use, but we will believe God is judging us as well. I like to call this the Matthew 7:2 principle. Matthew 7:2 is saying how we view and interact with people will reflect onto ourselves. This principle does not only apply to judgment and forgiveness, but in virtually any manner of interaction with another. This is the reason God tells us to forgive or we will not be forgiven (Mathew 6:15).

Matthew 6:15 (NIV): But if you do not forgive others their sins, your Father will not forgive your sins.

What most don't understand is that God is not saying we are not forgiven. When God's Word speaks of forgiveness, it is in the context to forgive because Christ has already forgiven us.

The Matthew 7:2 principle shows us that when we do not forgive others, we will believe that God is not forgiving us as well and will result in our failure to experience His perfect love. This is crucial because our ability to love others is contingent on our reception or belief of God's forgiveness of our sins (Luke 7:47).

In Colossians, we see that our sins have already been forgiven through believing in the crucifixion and

APPLICATION

The Matthew 7:2 principle not only applies to judging or forgiving others, but in manipulating others as well. If we are nice to someone to get something from them (manipulation), the next time someone is nice to us we will think they are being nice to get something from us.

Another example is if we lie to someone or do not trust them, we will always think that people are lying to us or do not trust us.

resurrection of Christ. In Hebrews 9:28, we know Christ was sacrificed once to take away the sins of *all* (Hebrews 9:28). The forgiveness of our sins has already taken place upon our belief of Jesus Christ as Lord and Savior (John 3:16).

Colossians 2:13 (KJV): And you, being dead in your sins and the *uncircumcision of your flesh, hath he quickened together with him, **having forgiven you all trespasses;***

Luke 7:47 shows us that our ability to love others is based on the degree of our understanding or receiving God's forgiveness of our sins.

Luke 7:47 shows us that our ability to love others is based on the degree of our understanding or receiving God's forgiveness of our sins.

Luke 7:47 (NIV): Therefore, I tell you, her many sins have been forgiven--as her great love has shown. But whoever has been forgiven little loves little."

This is an important principle in the finished works of Jesus that we need to understand. The more we believe God has forgiven our sins, and the more we experience Grace, the greater empowerment we will have to love others as Christ loves us (John 15:12). We need to believe it, receive it, and only then can we live out the perfect love that God not only has for us, but for the world as well.

THINKING POINT

Judgment has already taken place in the body of Christ. Our sins have already been forgiven. Understanding these concepts not only gives us the whole picture of God's perfect love for us, but they empower us to love others as Christ loves us (Luke 7:47, John 13:34, 15:12).

When you believe Christ has taken on your judgment and that your sins have been forgiven, think about how it will change how you interact with people, and how it will increase your ability to forgive others. It will also take away the power and authority others have to offend you. You will not be offended when you know God's love for you, because it will fulfill you, sustain you, and be all that matters.

3.4 SUPER-ABOUNDING GRACE

There are two doctrines that are criticized the most in the church today. I believe the enemy attacks them because they are the most empowering. These doctrines are praying in the Spirit, and the Gospel of Grace. We will address praying in the Spirit in the Chapter on Communication, and we will discuss Grace now.

People who preach radical Grace or "too much grace" are often criticized. Not so much radical Grace as in "everyone is going to be saved", because that is not true, but the Grace message that sins have been paid for past, present, and future. One cannot teach too much Grace. Grace is it--the meat and potatoes, the very foundation of the Cross and what Christ accomplished. Grace is the New

Covenant. We see this in John 1:17:

> John 1:17 (KJV): For the law was given by Moses, but grace and truth **came by Jesus Christ.**

The Greek word for "came" is ginomai (γίνομαι), and means, "to become; to come into existence". What is interesting is the way it's written in Greek makes grace and truth singular, meaning they are one. What John 1:17 is saying is that grace is the truth and the truth is grace and you can't separate the two!

Grace is the very will and plan of God to reconcile man to Himself (Ephesians 2:15), specifically, through Jesus Christ. Grace is the power of salvation and it is the empowerment of our lives in Christ. The definition of power is the ability to get results. When a Christian's life is 'not working' or lacking results, it is because they have not taken hold of the empowerment of Grace. And this can be very frustrating. You may be asking how grace is empowering? Let us take a look:

> Romans 1:16 (KJV): For I am not ashamed of the **gospel of Christ:** for it is the **power of God** unto salvation to everyone that **believeth;** to the Jew first, and also to the Greek.

The Gospel is the power of salvation, or the power of God to be saved, healed, delivered, preserved, prospered, protected, and made whole. These are the finished works of Jesus that have already been completed within us, available to manifest in our everyday life. These inheritances of salvation, these finished works of Jesus, means we have been made whole, for example, but we must learn how to live in His wholeness. The Gospel is the empowerment of salvation to manifest in our life upon our belief. So, what is the Gospel?

> Acts 20:24 (KJV): so that I might finish my course with joy, and the ministry, which I have received of the LORD Jesus, to testify the **gospel of the grace of God.**

In Acts 20:24 we see that the Gospel is specifically the Gospel of the Grace of God. In combining Romans 1:16 and Acts 20:24, we see that the Gospel of Grace is the empowerment (ability to get results) or the manifestation of salvation in our life.

> In Romans 1:16 and Acts 20:24, we see that the Gospel of Grace is the empowerment (ability to get results) or the manifestation of salvation in our life.

Therefore, the *empowerment* or the manifestation of the finished works of Jesus in our life, is *through Grace!* This is also why we know that whenever Jesus or the disciples were preaching the Gospel, they were preaching Grace and it resulted in the power of God manifesting in signs, miracles, and salvation!

Grace has 2 components. The first is that we have God's unmerited, undeserved, and unearned favor of God (Psalm 5:12, Luke 2:52, Romans 3:24). The second is that it is God who works for us, in us, and through us (Titus 2:12, Philippians 2:13, 2 Corinthians 12:9). When we hear preaching that isn't rooted in Grace, we are not hearing the Gospel. To hear the Gospel of Christ, the message has got to be rooted in Grace and will result in bondages being broken and healings manifesting.

Now then, what exactly is the Gospel of Grace? We have a problem of complicating the gospel. The gospel is simple such that children can understand:

> Colossians 1:22-23 (NIV): But now **he has** reconciled you by Christ's physical body through death to present you holy in his sight, without blemish **(faultless)** and free from accusation **(blameless)**— (23) if you continue in your faith, established and firm, and do not move from the hope held out in the gospel. **This is the gospel** that you heard and that has been proclaimed to every creature under heaven, and of which I, Paul, have become a servant.

The Gospel of the Grace of God is simply that through the blood of Christ being shed, we are:

1. Freely justified through Christ (Romans 3:24).
2. Faultless and blameless (Ephesians 1:4; Colossians 1:22).
3. Righteous and without blemish (Romans 1:17; Ephesians 5:27).

When the Bible speaks of the Gospel being preached, especially in the Book of Acts, it is almost always followed by "and their numbers grew". This is because the Gospel is attractive to everyone--the lost as well as the found. The Gospel is simple, easy to understand, and draws people to Christ. One of the biggest reasons why churches do not grow, is because the Gospel isn't being preached or we try and complicate it. We try and fancy it up or stick some bling on it to make it attractive, or to make ourselves sound smart and spiritual. Reality is that people will be drawn to the Gospel in its simplest and purest form, because it is the way, the truth and the life! We've been created to live in the Gospel of Grace.

In Ephesians 1:4 we see that it was God's original plan for us to be made pure and blameless. God knew this could only happen through Grace:

> Ephesians 1:4 (NIV): For he chose us in him before the creation of the world to be holy and blameless in his sight.

God's plan from the beginning of time was for us to have perfect communion with Him through relationship. The only way for this to happen was for Him to take the 'bad' out of us, and He did. God is not looking at us through a microscope, just waiting for us to mess up or to catch us being bad. God already knows we have been bad. In His infinite wisdom and knowledge, God devised a plan before the beginning of time to take the bad out of us. This is Grace, making us one with Christ or one humanity out of two.

> Ephesians 2:15 (NIV): His purpose was to create in himself one new humanity out of the two, thus making peace

Often, we don't see what God sees in us. We look in the mirror and we don't like what we see in the reflection. We look in the mirror and we see our past mistakes, bad decisions, our past hurts and pains, all resulting in an identity placed in our behaviors of the past.

But God doesn't see what we see. God sees us perfect, spotless, whole, and without blemish. He sees us this way because of the blood of Christ, and this is how He relates to us. Even though He knows our past sins and mistakes, He loves what He sees because He has created us perfectly. The past is the past, and what He sees now is a new creation! A perfect creation in Christ. When we look in the mirror and see ourselves as God does, our smile will be as big as His. Being without blemish, faultless, and blameless is our righteous standing in Christ:

> Romans 5:2 (NIV): through whom we have gained access by faith into this grace in which we now stand. And we boast in the hope of the glory of God.

THINKING POINT

Why do we always think that God is looking down at us with a magnifying glass to see if we are good or bad? God already knows we have been bad and is why He sent His perfect son to die on the Cross for the propitiation of sins.

Why is it so hard for us to believe that in all His infinite wisdom, power, and ability, God devised a plan to take the bad out of us? Taking the bad out of us is exactly what He did when He condemned our sinful flesh (Romans 8:3) and placed it on the body of Christ, exchanging Christs' righteousness for our sins.

It is important to understand the difference between our state and our standing. Our state is temporal, changing in accordance to our emotions, feelings, experiences, etc. Our standing, to the contrary, is permanent in Christ through Grace (Romans 5:2).

Too many times we get confused and believe God measures us by our temporary state. The truth is we are the ones measuring ourselves by our temporary state and attributing it to how God sees us.

Once we become a child of Grace, God always relates to us as He sees us in our perfect, spotless, blameless, and without blemish, righteous standing in Christ.

APPLICATION

When you look in the mirror, do you see what God sees? Do you see yourself as blameless, and without blemish?

That is how God sees you through Grace by the blood of Christ. You are one with Christ (Ephesians 2:15).

Each time you look in the mirror, speak God's Word over you. See yourself as God does and watch how it manifests through you! It will be life changing!

We must remember to judge ourselves by our state, understanding our need to

> **As a child of Grace, God always relates to us as He sees us in our perfect, spotless, blameless, without blemish standing in Christ.**

make changes or adjustments (sometimes just choosing not to be grumpy, for example) and measure ourselves by our righteous standing in Christ. This will change how we see ourselves, therefore giving us power over our state through the love of Christ.

Now that we understand the power of God's Word is Grace, we can understand that Grace is what breaks the bondages of sin in our life and not through our effort.

> *Romans 5:20-21 (KJV): Moreover the law entered, that the offence might abound. But where sin abounded, grace did much more abound: (21) That as sin hath reigned unto death, even so might grace reign through righteousness unto eternal life by Jesus Christ our LORD.*

Romans 5:20-21 shows us that no matter the sin or the amount of sin in our life, the grace of God is greater!

It is by the Grace of God that we have been delivered from the power of sin and not through our 'works', effort, or willpower (Zachariah 4:6, Titus 2:12, Philippians 2:13, 2 Corinthians 12:9). Since we have already been delivered from our sin, we need to learn how to live in our deliverance. If we try and live a righteous, sin-free life through our own willpower, we will fail and experience the frustration of a Christian life 'not working.'

2 WAYS TO RIGHTEOUSNESS

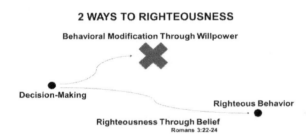

Behavioral Modification Through Willpower

Decision-Making

Righteous Behavior

Righteousness Through Belief
Romans 3:22-24

Do you remember our two ways to righteousness example back in Chapter One? This is what Grace does. Grace infects our heart with the love of God in that sinful behavior is not a part of our nature because sin will be unnatural to us.

Righteousness is a natural reaction to experiencing God's love, or Grace, and begins with right believing. Righteous fruits may take time. But as with any tree or plant, it takes time for the roots to become established; for the nutrients to work their way up the tree into the branches, producing fruit.

Our belief in Grace is our roots becoming established in the love of Christ and what He accomplished on the Cross. The place where Grace super-abounds over sin is in our heart. Grace, God's perfect love, produces change in our heart that leads to change in our nature or who we are, therefore, how we behave.

It is not a change that comes from behavioral modification through willpower, but through letting God's perfect love fulfill and complete us where nothing is missing or lacking. When we are filled with the fullness of God or His perfect love (Ephesians 3:19), sin will not be desired, logical, nor in our nature. And it starts with our beliefs. Right(eous) believing leads to right(eous) living (Romans 3:22).

The place where Grace super-abounds over sin is in our heart. Grace, God's perfect love, produces change in our heart that leads to a change in our nature or who we are, therefore, how we behave.

REAL LIFE

Justin had a strong addiction to sexual promiscuity before God radically and supernaturally healed his life. Justin was not faithful to a single woman his entire life. His transformation and empowerment came through God's grace, followed by the gift of God his wife, Renee. When Justin and Renee began to realize they were interested in one another after his was transformed, Justin started to freak out because he did not know if he could trust himself to be faithful to Renee, whom he valued and deeply respected. Justin was perplexed by God's timing because he finally arrived at a place in his life where he was free from addictions, and he was able to intimately pursue the presence of God without distractions. Justin was happy being single and alone with God for the first time in his life. In fact, the last thing he wanted in life, was a woman!

After Justin experienced healing from what he struggled with the most, women, God had sent him a woman who had never been with another man before. After praying and fasting to ensure this was truly God's will, Justin experienced the true power of God's grace. Women were his kryptonite. They were the most difficult area of his life that he could not control, more so than alcoholism. Because of Grace, Justin had the self-control to abstain from even touching Renee for the first five months of their relationship. This man who had objectified and lusted after women for over two decades of his life, was free from impure, sexual thoughts and motives towards Renee. Where Justin was weak in sin, the empowerment of God's Grace gave him strength to overcome, to respect Renee and have a pure relationship with her through marriage that continues to this day. Sin was conquered because the desire was conquered in the fullness of God's perfect love. That is grace (Titus 2:12, Philippians 2:13, 2 Corinthians 12:9).

INDIVIDUAL/GROUP DISCUSSION QUESTIONS

1. Sovereign means "one who exercises supreme authority within a limited sphere" (Merriam-Webster). What is God 'limited' to? (John 1:1, James 1:17; p.31)

_____

_____

_____

_____

2. Explain why the law of goodness is in God's nature and character; that it is within His "limited sphere of sovereignty", (John 1:1, James 4:17; p.34)

    _____
    _____
    _____
    _____

3. If the sins of the world have been paid for by Christ, why do people go to hell? (p.36-37)

    _____
    _____
    _____
    _____

4. Explain the Matthew 7:2 principle in your own words. (Matthew 7:2; p.39)

    _____
    _____
    _____
    _____

    How do we know that the Truth of God's Word and Grace are one? (John 1:17, p.41)

    _____
    _____
    _____
    _____

5. What is the simple, basic definition of the Gospel of the Grace of God? (Acts 20:24, Colossians 1:22-23; p.42)

    _____
    _____
    _____
    _____

6. Why will a child of Grace never experience the wrath of God? (Romans 5:1, Ephesians 2:15)

    _____
    _____
    _____
    _____

7. In your own words, explain the difference between God's wrath and judgment, and the natural consequences of sin. Are they the same thing? (Romans 6:23)

    _____
    _____
    _____
    _____

CHAPTER 4

THE LAW MADE OBSOLETE

4.1 THE OPPOSITE OF GRACE

In continuing to establish our beliefs in the truth of God's Word, we will continue our discussion on beliefs with a further understanding of Grace. To really understand Grace, which is our underserved, unmerited, and unearned favor of God as well as God working for us, in us, and through us, we will look to its opposite.

> *Romans 11:6 (KJV): And if by grace, then is it no more of works: otherwise grace is no more grace.*

> *Galatians 5:4 (NIV): You who are trying to be justified by the law have been alienated from Christ; you have fallen away from grace.*

In putting together Romans 11:6 and Galatians 5:4, the opposite of Grace is works, and specifically, the law. The reason Grace is the opposite of 'works', or the law, is because it is through the Grace of God that we are freely justified by our faith and belief in Christ (Romans 3:22) and not through our obedience to the law.

> **The reason Grace is the opposite of 'works' is because it is through the Grace of God that we are freely justified by our faith and belief in Christ.**

The reason this 'works' or law mentality is a problem is because we are trying to obtain righteousness or justification through what we do (our works) rather than freely receiving it from God. Living under this law mentality not only manifests as literally striving to follow the Ten Commandments (living under the Old Covenant), but also through feelings of having to perform good works in a desperate attempt to earn a right standing with God (righteousness). We are trying to obtain righteousness by ourselves, or self-righteousness, which is the purest form of unrighteousness. If we had the ability to obtain righteousness through our works, Christ would not have needed to die on the Cross because we would be able to follow the Ten Commandments perfectly. This 'works' mentality will always fail because no matter how many good 'works' we do, they will only be good enough until the next time we sin, leading to condemnation, guilt, and shame. We will never feel justified with God and it will lead to burnout, frustration, anger, bitterness towards God, and even leaving the Christian faith. And, more importantly, it is a rejection of Grace, or what God has freely given us through the sacrifice of Jesus Christ.

Freely receiving Grace will naturally produce righteous fruits or good 'works', like serving at church or giving financially. The motivation is different in that it is from a heart filled with the love of Jesus, His nature becoming ours, motivating our behaviors. The point we need to make is that there is a drastic difference in good 'works' as a means to achieving self-righteousness, in comparison to the natural fruits of righteousness that comes from belief and faith in Jesus Christ:

> *Romans 3:20-24 (NIV): Therefore no one will be declared righteous in God's sight by the works of the law; rather, through the law we become conscious of our sin. (21) But now apart from the law the righteousness of God has been made known, to which the law and the Prophets testify. (22) This righteousness **is given through faith in Jesus Christ to all who believe.** There is no difference between Jew and Gentile, (23) For all have sinned and fall short of the glory of God, (24) and **all are justified freely by his grace** through the redemption that came by Christ Jesus.*

THINKING POINT

Religion teaches us that we have to do enough good 'works' to get into God's good standing. The Gospel teaches us that we are freely justified by faith and belief in Jesus Christ. This is the message of Grace. If we had the ability to follow the Ten Commandments or the law perfectly, we would be able to achieve righteousness by our own works or ability. There would be no reason for Jesus to have come as the Messiah, nor a need for Him to have died on the Cross.

What are the motives for your good 'works?' Do you do them to make you look good and 'spiritual' at church, or because God's love is overflowing in you and His nature has become yours?

The law is based on performance or 'works.' Grace is the opposite of performance because God loves us just as we are (Romans 5:8). We must believe we are the righteousness of God through Christ, and righteous deeds will be a natural result of our righteous nature in Christ rather than a means to obtain self-righteousness.

We must believe we are the righteousness of God through Christ, and righteous deeds will be a natural result of our righteous nature in Christ rather than a means to obtain self-righteousness.

Religion has taught us that we've got to be good enough for God's goodness, that there is nothing 'free'. God knows we are not good enough and is the reason He has freely given us Grace.

Because of His undeserved, unmerited, and unearned favor, we can freely obtain His goodness and love through simply believing in Him. When we turn to our 'works', or the law, to obtain righteousness, we minimize the power of Grace and we place ourselves under the curse of the law.

> *Galatians 3:10: For all who **rely on the works** of the law are under a curse, as it is written: "Cursed is everyone who does not continue to do **everything** written in the Book of the law.*

> Sin has power over us through the law. As long as we focus on what we're doing wrong rather than who we are in Christ, we will never be free from sin.

In Galatians 3:10, we see that it was the law that brought the curse of death to us through sin. Sin has power over us through the law. As long as we focus on what we're doing wrong rather than who we are in Christ, we will never be free from sin.

Romans 7:9-11 (KJV): For I was alive without the law once: but when the commandment came, sin revived, and I died. (10) And the commandment, which was ordained to life, I found to be death. (11) For sin, taking occasion by the commandment, deceived me, and by it slew me.

If the law is a curse to us, why did God send it? Well, if there was no law there would be no sin. For example, if there was no law to regulate the speed limit, the act of speeding would not exist.

Romans 4:15 (KJV): Because the law worketh wrath: for where no law is, there is no transgression.

The law was also given to show us that sin had dominion over us before the crucifixion, hence the curse, to show us our need for a Savior.

Romans 6:14-15 (KJV): For sin shall not have dominion over you: for ye are not under the law, but under grace.

Galatians 3:24 (KJV): Wherefore the law was our schoolmaster to bring us unto Christ, that we might be justified by faith.

> The law was given to show us that sin had dominion over us before the crucifixion, hence the curse, to show us our need for a Savior.

The law was brought to show us our need for a Savior because we are incapable of attaining righteousness through our 'works'. If God had never given us the law, when Jesus came as our Savior, we would have looked at Him like He was nuts because we would have had no idea we needed a Savior.

The law was given to show us our need for a Savior by making us conscious of sin. Being sin-conscious is also why the law is a curse in that it brings sin to life (Romans 7:9-11), therefore produces sin (Romans 4:15), and the wages of sin is death, and death is eternal separation from God (Romans 6:23).

> What a lot of us fail to realize is that sin is revived in our life when we are conscious of it.

What a lot of us fail to realize is that sin is revived in our life when we are conscious of it. Focusing on sin will result in its continued manifestation through our behavior. You tell a child not to lick a lollipop, guess what they're going to do?

This is the reason it is crucial not to be sin-conscious, but Grace-conscious. In fact, in the next few chapters we will see how God's blood cleanses our conscience. Grace has redeemed us from the curse of the law making the law obsolete, freeing us from guilt and shame and the bondages of sin.

> Galatians 3:13 (NIV): Christ redeemed us from the curse of the law by becoming a curse for us.

> Romans 6:14 (NIV): For sin shall not be master over you, for you are not under law but under grace.

APPLICATION

When you think about your relationship with God throughout your day, how much time is devoted to being critical of your behavior? Do you focus on not sinning or trying not to sin?

Rather than focusing on your behavior, change your focus to God's love for you. You are freely justified through the blood of Christ. Think about what He has freely given you through Grace and watch your confidence grow in righteousness!

When we are weak and struggling with sin is precisely the time to come boldly into God's presence, to His throne of Grace, and receive strength to overcome.

> Hebrews 4:16 (NIV): Let us then approach God's throne of grace with confidence, so that we may receive mercy and find grace to help us in our time of need.

When we are conscious of the law or sin-conscious, it produces condemnation and guilt which prevents us from boldly entering God's presence during the times we need to the most. Being that Grace prevails or super-abounds over sin in our heart, and the opposite of Grace is the law, I think it is important for us to understand why and how the law has been made obsolete.

When we are weak and struggling is precisely the time to come boldly into God's presence, to His throne of Grace, and receive strength to overcome.

4.2 WHY AND HOW THE LAW IS OBSOLETE

Now that we understand why Grace is the opposite of the law, we can understand that it is God's Grace that redeemed us from the curse of the law (the Old Covenant) by making it obsolete. Let us look at this Biblically:

> Hebrews 8:13 (NIV): By calling this covenant "new," he has made the first one obsolete; and what is obsolete and outdated will soon disappear.

> Colossians 2:14 (NIV): Blotting out the handwriting of ordinances that was against us, which was contrary to us, and took it out of the way, nailing it to his cross;

What are the "handwriting of ordinances" in Colossians 2:14? Hints:

1.   What did God write with His hand?
2.   What did God write onto stone with His finger?

The answer is the Ten Commandments.

> *Deuteronomy 9:10 (NIV): The LORD gave me two stone tablets inscribed by the finger of God. On them were all the commandments the LORD proclaimed to you on the mountain out of the fire, on the day of the assembly.*

THINKING POINT

Why was it God's Will to create the New Covenant?

1.   The Old Covenant (the law) was based on our ability to keep it perfectly, which is impossible (Hebrews 8:9).
2.   Sin was only covered; it did not take sin away (Hebrews 10:4).
3.   The law can't make us perfect (Hebrews 10:1-3).
4.   The law alienates us from Christ in that we fall from grace (Galatians 5:4).

The reason the law was made obsolete was because it was not able to make us righteous or in right-standing with God. The law was based on our ability to keep it, and we can't. The law has been made obsolete because there is a new way to righteousness rather than perfectly obeying the Ten Commandments, which is impossible.

> *Romans 3:22: This righteousness is given through faith in Jesus Christ to all who believe.*

> *Galatians 3:24-25: So the law was our guardian until Christ came that we might be justified by faith. (25)Now*

APPLICATION

Have you ever used the Ten Commandments to guide your behavior? I remember when it used to be posted in our schools and I would freak out when I failed to keep a commandment. I specifically remember sitting in Kindergarten thinking God was angry at me, feeling unworthy to pray to Him as I starred at the Ten Commandments.

Now I am relieved to know that is not the case, that we have the Holy Spirit within us to empower us to live righteously. Rather than focusing on your behavior, focus on God and watch your behavior follow!

that this faith has come, we are no longer under a guardian.

> **The Old Covenant or the Ten Commandments were never intended to make us righteous, but to show us our need for a Savior.**

The New Covenant is based on Grace, making us righteous through faith and belief in Christ. The New Covenant is based on Christ's ability to keep it and He's perfect.

Hebrews 9:15 (NIV): For this reason Christ is the mediator of a new covenant, that those who are called may receive the promised eternal inheritance--now that he has died as a ransom to set them free from the sins committed under the first covenant.

Now that we understand the 'why' of the Old Covenant being made obsolete, let us understand the 'how.' The Old Covenant or the Ten Commandments were never intended to make us righteous, but to show us our need for a Savior. Because we could not remain faithful to the Old Covenant, Christ came to mediate a new one that was not based on our ability to keep it, but on His ability, which is perfect.

In understanding 'how' the Law was made obsolete, we need to backtrack a bit. Upon salvation, we get a new spirit and a new heart, and something gets written on this new heart of ours.

> *Ezekiel 36:26 (NIV): I will give you a new heart and put a new spirit in you; I will remove from you your heart of stone and give you a heart of flesh.*

> *Jeremiah 31:33 (NIV): This is the covenant I will make with the people of Israel after that time," declares the LORD. "I will put **my law** in their minds and write it on their hearts. I will be their God, and they will be my people.*

If you remember, Jesus summed up the Old Covenant, or the law, in Mark 12:30-31, as to love others as we love ourselves.

> *Mark 12:30-31 (NIV): 'Love the LORD your God with all your heart and with all your soul and with all your mind and with all your strength.' (31) The second is this: 'Love your neighbor **as yourself**.' There is no commandment greater than these."*

I am sure you agree that we are not always the best at loving ourselves. Because of the New Covenant and the empowerment of the Holy Spirit upon salvation, we now are able to love others as *Christ loves us*. This is the "my law" in Jeremiah 31:33, also known as the new command in John 13:34 and 15:12.

> *John 13:34: A new command I give you: Love one another. **As I have loved you**, so you must love one another.*

> *John 15:12: My command is this: Love each other **as I have loved you**.*

> **Our ability to love others depends on how much we let God forgive us.**

Our ability to love is contingent on our ability to receive God's forgiveness (Luke 7:47). Our ability to love is not based on our effort, for if we're under 'works' we are not under grace (Romans 11:6).

Our ability to love others is contingent on our ability to let God forgive us. In other words, as we learned earlier, our ability to love others depends on how much we believe God has forgiven our sins, or our ability to receive *Grace!*

> *Luke 7:47: "I tell you, her sins--and they are many--have been forgiven, so she has shown me much love. But a person who is forgiven little shows only little love."*

Our ability to love is based on living a Holy Spirit-influenced life and this is how the law is fulfilled in us, making it obsolete. When we do not accept God's forgiveness, we feel unworthy to be in His presence or filled with the Spirit (because we are sin-conscious), inhibiting our ability to love others as Christ loves us (John 13:34).

> *Romans 8:3-4 (KJV): For what the Law could not do, weak as it was through the flesh, God did: sending His own Son in the likeness of sinful flesh and as an offering for sin, He condemned sin in the flesh, (4) so that* **the requirement of the Law might be fulfilled in us, who do not walk according to the flesh but according to the Spirit.**

In His perfect love, there is no consciousness of sin freeing us to be sensitive to the Spirit rather than full of guilt and shame.

Fulfilling the law is living in God's love through a Holy Spirit-influenced life (Romans 8:4). In His perfect love there is no consciousness of sin freeing us to be sensitive to the Spirit rather than full of guilt and shame. Sensitivity to the Spirit allows God's love to manifest through us into the world.

There is one crucial component we need to remember when speaking of the law being made obsolete or being fulfilled in us:

> *Colossians 2:13-15 (KJV): And you, being dead in your sins and the uncircumcision of your flesh, hath he quickened together with him, having forgiven you all trespasses; (14) Blotting out the handwriting of ordinances that was against us, which was contrary to us, and took it out of the way, nailing it to his cross; (15)* **And** *having spoiled principalities and powers, he made a shew of them openly, triumphing over them in it.*

Notice how right after the law was blotted out in 2 Corinthians 2:14-15, it goes right to the defeat of the kingdom of darkness. Do you think there is a reason? Let us see if we can find a clue in Revelation 12:

Notice how right after the law was blotted out in 2 Corinthians 2:14-15, it goes right to the defeat of the kingdom of darkness.

Revelation 12:9-11: And the great dragon was cast out, that old serpent, called the Devil, and Satan, which deceiveth the whole world: he was cast out into the earth, and his angels were cast out with him. (10) And I heard a loud voice saying in heaven, Now is come salvation, and strength, and the kingdom of our God, and the power of his Christ: for the **accuser** *of our brethren is cast down, which* **accused** *them before our God day and* *night. (11) And they overcame him by the blood of the Lamb, and by the word of their testimony; and they loved not their lives unto the death.*

In Revelation 12:10, we see that the accuser is Satan. What did Satan accuse the brethren with? The answer is the law or the "handwriting of ordinances" in Colossians 2:14.

Being that God has given us dominion over the earth (Genesis 1:26) and has stripped Satan of his powers and principalities (Colossians 2:15), the only weapon Satan can use against us are lies that we choose to believe. Satan's primary goal is to get us to believe that we are not worthy enough for a relationship with God. If you remember, this is the barrier of inaccurate beliefs that we discussed in Chapter 1, Section 1.2, when we translated 2 Corinthians 10:5.

The only means Satan had to accuse us with (the law) has been made obsolete by the blood of Christ (Revelations 12:11). If we have been given dominion over the earth and Satan has been stripped of power and principalities through the law being made obsolete, the only authority the enemy has in our life is the authority we give him.

The reason the blood of Christ is so powerful in our lives is because it answers *every* accusation and lie Satan throws at us to bring on condemnation and a guilty sin-conscience. We are covered by the blood of the Lamb.

If we have been given domain over the earth and the enemy has been stripped of power and principalities, the only authority the enemy has in our life is the authority we give him.

APPLICATION

Did you know that your righteous behavior will come to fruit by focusing on the Holy Spirit rather than being critical of yourself? The law is fulfilled in you and not through your willpower to follow the Ten Commandments, but through your desire to seek God first and being sensitive to the Holy Spirit.

So, rather than focusing on your behavior, focus on your sensitivity to the still, small voice of the Holy Spirit.

THINKING POINT

The lies of Satan are the same accusations that the law makes of us: That we do not deserve what God has given us (Grace) through the crucifixion of Christ.

Next time you feel guilty for what you have done or not worthy to be in God's presence, realize this is a lie from Satan and that God loves you so much that He shed the perfect blood of His Son, Jesus Christ, that you would be made perfect, blameless, faultless, and without blemish (Ephesians 1:4, 5:27, Colossians 1:22).

REAL LIFE

Being that God has given us dominion over the earth (Genesis 1:26) and has stripped Satan of his powers and principalities (Colossians 2:15), why do we need the armor of God? Why do we need to stand up to Satan if he has already been defeated?

Think of it this way. Justin weighed around 250 lbs., was a bouncer for almost seven years, and a cage fighter for almost two years while training in mixed martial arts and lifting weights regularly. The point being, he clearly had power over a six-year old girl. However, despite his past experiences, training, and strength, if he gave the six-year old the opportunity, she could kick him in the shin and cause tremendous pain. In fact, if he did nothing at all and she was instructed properly, she could kill him. This happened one night when he successfully trained his friends daughter how to put him in a rear-naked-choke hold. She performed it successfully, cutting of the circulation to his brain (I had to tap out)!

This is the reason we need to arm ourselves with the belt of truth, the breastplate of righteousness, the shoes of peace, the shield of faith, and the helmet of salvation (Ephesians 6). By being armed with the armor of God, we are not giving the kingdom of darkness an opportunity to inflict fear and doubt in our lives.

4.3 LIVING IN WILLFUL SIN

When talking about Christ taking on our judgment at the Cross, that our sins, past, present, and future are paid for along with the law being fulfilled in us through living a Holy Spirit-influenced life, we need to know why we don't have a free pass to sin.

A main reason why Grace is not taught in churches today is for fear that people will believe they are free to sin because sins have already been forgiven (Hebrews 2:17, 9:15, 9:28). This same argument of sinning freely is what Paul faced and addressed when he wrote Romans 6 and is one reason why we know Paul preached radical Grace.

When Paul was asked in Romans 6:1 if we should go on sinning that Grace may increase, Paul's response was, "How?" In other words, Paul asked how it was possible for one to keep on sinning once they have experienced Grace, or God's perfect love? When one experiences Grace, sin is not natural or in their nature because they will have the nature and character of God himself (1 John 4:17). The more time we spend in

> Even though sin has been paid for, there remains real and natural consequences to sin that we will experience as well as those around us.

God's presence, the more His passions become ours and the more sin will not be enticing or natural to us.

Even though sin has been paid for, there remains real and natural consequence to sin that we will experience as well as those around us. Jesus satisfied God's judgment of sin, not the natural consequences of it in this fallen world. We need to understand the destructiveness of sin aside from the natural consequences of it. Sin is destructive because willful sin is deceptive sin.

> Hebrews 3:13 (KJV): But exhort one another daily, while it is called today; lest any of you be hardened through the deceitfulness of sin.

Sin's deceitfulness means that we don't realize the damage sin does in our life, because we are insensitive or ignorant to its consequences.

Sin's deceitfulness means we don't realize the damage sin does in our life because we are insensitive or ignorant to its consequences, so to speak. The problem with sin other than it leading to death (Romans 6:23) is that, when done willingly, it progressively hardens our Heart making us insensitive to the Holy Spirit and the power of God's Grace.

If we experience conviction when we sin, we are not under the deception of sin because we see sin for what it is through the conviction (instruction into righteousness) of the Holy Spirit, leading to repentance (changing our mind, therefore behavior). This is one of the reasons why living in willful sin is so dangerous and destructive. We do not realize how sin is hardening our heart until it has already happened, resulting in our insensitivity to the Spirit.

Remember, when we choose to believe in Christ as LORD and Savior, we are given a new spirit and a heart of flesh. In combining Ezekiel 36:26 and Hebrews 3:13, we can deduce that a stony heart is associated with being spiritually dead because when we are born again (salvation), our stony heart is replaced with a heart of flesh.

> Ezekiel 36:26 (NIV): I will give you a new heart and put a new spirit in you; I will remove from you your heart of stone and give you a heart of flesh.

> Hebrews 3:13 (KJV): But exhort one another daily, while it is called today; lest any of you be hardened through the deceitfulness of sin.

The link between these two verses is a stony heart and a hardened heart. We see in Ezekiel 36:26 that the Hebrew word for a stony heart is "'eben" (אֶבֶן), and means, "a perverse, hard heart". The definition of perverse is "turned away from what is right or good: corrupt, improper, or incorrect".

If willful sin creates a hardened heart, and a stony or hard heart is associated with being spiritually dead, we can logically and scripturally reason that willful sin will inevitably lead to a spiritually death-like

If willful sin creates a hardened heart, and a stony heart is associated with being spiritually dead, we can logically and scripturally reason that willful sin will inevitably lead to a spiritually death-like state.

state, or rather, spiritual insensitivity to God through the hardening of our heart.

When we say that a believer is spiritually dead-like, we are referring to their insensitivity to God's love and presence due to a hardened heart, much like an unbeliever who is spiritually dead or separated from God before salvation.

In contrast to a stony or wicked heart is a heart of flesh; a heart that is soft and warm--a heart which can be formed, molded, tenderized, developed, taught, matured, and worked on. It is pliable. It is a heart that is sensitive to the Holy Spirit. It is a heart that is after God's own. And if you remember, God is so intimately involved in everyday life that He guides our steps (Proverbs 16:9, Psalm 37:23). If we are spiritually insensitive to God's direction, how can we follow His lead into healing, deliverance, prosperity, protection, preservation, and wholeness (the seven definitions of salvation)? This hardening of heart can be what happens to those who feel they are 'distant' or 'separated' from God.

It is not that God is not with them or not working in their life, they are simply spiritually insensitive to His presence. Spiritual insensitivity does not always happen solely due to sin. It can happen just through our focus being on the world or our circumstances more so than God's presence and love. Remember, a hardened heart is insensitive to the Spirit, and fulfilling the law in Romans 8:4 is living a Holy Spirit-influenced life. Being sensitive to the Spirit is crucial in being sensitive to God directing our steps to live everyday life in His perfect love.

This state of insensitivity to the Spirit has nothing to do with God leaving or loving us less but has everything to do with the condition of our heart. We stop experiencing His love because we have believed the lie of sin (its deceitfulness). Living in sin closes our heart to receiving God's perfect love through knowing His presence. Therefore, we fail to live in knowing who we are in Christ and His direction for what He has purposed for our lives. We will wander in the desert.

> 2 Corinthians 12:9 (KJV): "And he said unto me, My grace is sufficient for thee: for my strength is made perfect in weakness.

REAL LIFE

Renee experienced such an extreme season of hardness of heart that she believed she had lost her salvation and was condemned to hell. And as a young woman, the light in her eyes went out and the hope in her heart barely beat. The sweet, full-of-life little girl who loved Jesus with all her heart didn't know how much He loved her. This was not because God stopped loving her, nor was it due to "sins" that many would attribute to the hardening of heart. It came from the sin of trying to earn God's love, or self-righteousness. It came from living under the law; from not understanding God's grace--that He loved her unconditionally. Righteousness, right standing before God, is a gift in Jesus and not something to be earned by our "good works". Renee was sincere in her efforts, but we can be sincere and sincerely wrong at the same time.

No one knew how driven Renee was to earn God's love, not even herself. From her limited perspective, and tainted estimation, there was just something wrong with her and she best get it together and keep it together. For a decade, she tried with a genuine heart to be right and do right for God, but this law-mentality was a relentless and ugly way to live. Renee's heart finally broke under the weight of all that she tried to carry in earning God's righteousness. She became severely depressed, malnourished, and was hospitalized for suicidal ideation. There was no wiggle room; no breath left. Her soul was fragmented after she tried to live out the 'perfect' Christian life, whatever that is, without knowing God's perfect love for her regardless of her performance. What kept Renee from taking her own life was the literal fear of going to hell.

In multiple ways Renee was brought back to life, April of 2010, through learning the truth of God's nature and character, and through the love of the body of Christ. It was the sweetest taste that set all her senses ablaze! Everything was so beautiful. Everything was better than new. Her heart was on an absolute high because she finally was experiencing God's perfect love that she had longed and labored to know for over a decade. And she was bathed in it; an unconditional love so strong that it healed places inside of her that she could never put words to and no man could touch. In her worst state, incapable of doing one thing for herself, especially the "Christian to-do-list", she experienced the purest and sweetest encounter with the power of God's grace that set her so free she could only feel His peace and love.

INDIVIDUAL/GROUP DISCUSSION QUESTIONS

1. Why is a 'works' mentality the same thing as living under the law?
    (Romans 11:6, Galatians 5:4; p.47)

    _____

    _____

    _____

    _____

2. Being that the law is made obsolete because it is fulfilled, how is it fulfilled
    in us? (Romans 8:4)

    _____

    _____

    _____

    _____

3. Explain why the only authority the enemy has in our life is the authority we give him. (Genesis 1:26, Colossians 2:15; p.54)

_____

_____

_____

_____

4. How is there power in the blood of Christ and how do we apply it in our life, today? (Colossians 2:13-15; p.54)

_____

_____

_____

_____

5. Why is having a stony heart, characteristic of our spiritually dead-like state before salvation, similar to having a hard heart that is characteristic of being insensitive to the Holy Spirit? (p.56-57)

_____

_____

_____

_____

6. Explain in your own words why living in willful sin is destructive. (Hebrews 3:13; p.56)

_____

_____

_____

_____

CHAPTER 5

A CLEANSED CONSCIENCE

5.1 THE LAW PROBLEM

Despite the law being made obsolete, the law is perfect and good because it has been originated by a perfect God. Although the law is a vital part of God's plan today, post-crucifixion, it creates problems for believers because it is not understood. This may be hard to believe due to religion using the law to manipulate believers into obedience; the law is not meant for us to live by, to be conscious of, or even to use (Galatians 5:4; 1 Timothy 1:9).

> *1 Timothy 1:9 (KJV): Knowing this, that the law is not made for a righteous man, but for the lawless and disobedient, for the ungodly and for sinners, for unholy and profane.*

The law is not meant for us to live by, to be conscious of, or even to use.

> *Galatians 5:4 (NIV): You who are trying to be justified by the law have been alienated from Christ; you have fallen away from grace.*

As 1 Timothy states, the law is not for the righteous. We are given a superior way and empowerment to righteousness and that is through faith and belief in Jesus Christ and living a Holy Spirit-*influenced* life (Romans 3:22; 8:4). The reason to speak so strongly on God's perfect law is that it needs to be understood the way God has designed it. When misunderstood, the law is a curse (Galatians 3:13). Religion has perverted the use of the law, using it as a means of motivation through trying to scare or manipulate believers into giving, serving, or 'holy living'.

THINKING POINT

As we discussed last chapter, if the law is what Satan uses to accuse us, why would we look to the law to guide our behaviors rather than the Holy Spirit within us? Is not the direction of the Holy Spirit superior to the Ten Commandments?

For example, concerning marriage, the law only tells us not to commit adultery. The Spirit, however, gives us the ability and direction to love our spouse as Christ loves the Church, naturally empowering us to be faithful. The influence of the Spirit directs and empowers us into righteousness in all aspects of life (Titus 12:2, Philippians 2:13), much superior to the law. This is the reason it is through living in the Spirit that the law is fulfilled in us, therefore obsolete (Romans 8:4)

The problem with living under the law, other than its curse, is that it ingrains a mentality that God is obligated to credit us as righteous because of the 'works' we do in our attempt to fulfill the law. This perverted understanding of the law will keep us from being free through Grace, in that we are kept in bondage to a 'works' mentality. We will never feel justified or good enough for God because we will only 'feel' justified until the next time we sin. This will be an exhausting, frustrating cycle because living in a 'works' mentality, or under the law, produces toxicity from stress and fear in trying to keep the law. It will literally kill us in that stress is the cause of 90-95% of sickness and disease, according to the federal Center for Disease Control, and is why the law is called the curse. This is the law problem.

The law problem is the mentality instilled by religion that gets us to think: 'If I do enough good things, God will spare me punishment', or 'If I do this, God has got to do that'. This is the obligation principle (Romans 4:4). When we stop trying to achieve righteousness by 'works' and trust in what Christ accomplished on the Cross, we are walking in faith. And rather than righteous behavior being a product of behavioral modification through willpower, our righteous behavior will be a natural result of living in God's perfect love that manifests through us into the world.

Righteousness is by belief and faith in Jesus Christ (Romans 3:22). David caught a prophetic glimpse of this righteousness through faith (Grace) when he wrote Psalm 31:

APPLICATION

Next time you think God is watching you to see if you mess up, remember that God has seen all your sins past, present, and future. He has already judged and executed them in the body of Christ.

God lives in an eternal realm void of time (Psalm 90:4, 2 Peter 3:8). He has already seen your life from beginning to end. Every day of your life has been written in His book (Psalm 139:16). God loves you so much that He has taken the 'bad' out of you and placed it on the body of Christ that He would see you in Christ, perfect and without blemish.

> *Romans 4:6-8 (NIV): David says the same thing when he speaks of the blessedness of the man to whom God credits righteousness apart from works: (7) "Blessed are they whose transgressions are forgiven, whose sins are covered. (8) Blessed is the man whose sin the LORD will never count against them"* (Psalm 31:1-2).

You might think, "Well, it says you have to be blessed." Well, we are blessed:

> *Ephesians 1:3 (NIV): Praise be to the God and Father of our LORD Jesus Christ, who **has blessed** us in the heavenly realms with **every** spiritual blessing in Christ.*

We have been blessed with *every* spiritual blessing (seven definitions of salvation)! The result of the New Covenant or the Gospel of Grace is us being made without blemish. In other words, as far as God is concerned, our sins don't exist!

> *Colossians 2:13 (KJV): And you, being dead in your sins and the uncircumcision of your flesh, hath he quickened together with him, having*

*forgiven you **all** trespasses.*

In Colossians 2:13, when does it say our sins are forgiven? The answer is when two become one, meaning when we become one with Christ through our death and resurrection in Him (salvation). This passage is speaking of salvation. And in the same verse, how many sins are forgiven? The answer, my friend, is *all of them!*

THINKING POINT

Why do we think we have the capability to pay for our sins? People have come to me sharing their pleas, bargaining for God to spare them the consequences of their actions in exchange for serving in the church, giving money, or volunteering for a mission trip, for some examples. One woman told God that if He kept her from getting pregnant, she would serve in children's ministry. She was essentially trying to pay for her sin by doing something for God to keep from experiencing a natural consequence (result) of pre-marital sex. The wages for sin is death (Romans 6:23).

My response to them is always the question of why we think we can afford to pay for sin? Is the crucifixion and death of Jesus Christ not enough? Do we have anything greater to offer God than the perfect blood of Christ? God is not looking for us to pay for our sins because that is a debt we cannot afford. He is looking for our belief in Jesus Christ, who paid for our sins, so we would be empowered through the Holy Spirit to live above sin and have relationship with Him. That is how much He loves us. That is Grace.

5.2 WITHOUT BLEMISH

If the Gospel of Grace is about obtaining righteousness by behavioral modification through willpower, or through our own ability, then Jesus did not have to die. The power to be sinless would be inside of us and we would be able to follow the Ten Commandments perfectly. But we cannot. That being said, over a billion dollars are spent every year in the Christian industry on "self-help" books to deal with sin. The false belief that we can conquer sin through our willpower is the reason we remain in bondage; never overcoming the sin that controls our life. People desire to stop sinning, but they are looking to the wrong solution. They are looking to the knowledge of books and their own ability when the solution is already inside of them: The Holy Spirit.

When we ask God to work on our sin, we are asking Him to work on the part of us that has been condemned and crucified in Christ (Romans 8:3, Galatians 2:20). We essentially try and raise our old, dead, stinking, rotting, decaying self from the grave when we try and will sinless behavior (behavior modification through willpower).

Romans 8:3-4 (NIV): For what the law was powerless to do because it was weakened by the flesh, God did by sending his own Son in the likeness of sinful flesh to be a sin offering. And so he condemned sin in the flesh, (4) in order that the righteous requirement of the law might be fully met in us, who do not live according to the flesh but according to the Spirit.

Romans 8:3-4 is speaking of us being crucified and resurrected with Christ upon salvation (Galatians 2:20), which is the whole 'born again' doctrine and the symbolism of baptism. For this discussion, we need to understand that Romans 8:3 says something very crucial: "He *condemned* sin in the flesh."

> **When we ask God to work on our sin, we are asking Him to work on the part of us that has been condemned and crucified in Christ.**

Where does sin originate from? Our flesh.

Romans 7:18 (NIV): For I know that good itself does not dwell in me, that is, in my sinful nature. For I have the desire to do what is good, but I cannot carry it out.

Sin originates from our sinful nature (or flesh) and manifests as thoughts and behaviors. It is important to understand that our sinful flesh (or nature) has been condemned and our sins have been forgiven (Colossians 2:13). Condemned means judged and executed. God condemned our sinful flesh in the body of Christ, meaning our sinful flesh has been judged and executed on the Cross, dying with Christ.

> **If our sins have been forgiven and our sinful flesh condemned in the body of Christ, what else is left to see other than our perfection in Christ?**

What God condemns He doesn't see because it has been judged and executed. Remember, God lives in a realm void of time (Psalm 90:4, 139:16, 2 Peter 3:8). He sees all our past, present, and future sins already placed on the body of Christ, forgiven and paid in full (Colossians 2:13). If our sins have been forgiven and our sinful flesh condemned in the body of Christ, what else is left to see other than our perfection in Christ?

God sees us as a new creation, without blemish, pure, perfect, faultless, and blameless. All the 'bad' in us has been judged and executed in the body of Christ. When God looks at us, He sees Christ because our sinful flesh has died with Christ and we have been resurrected in Him.

APPLICATION

Romans 12:2 (NIV): Do not conform to the patterns of the world, but be transformed by the renewing of your mind.

How many times a day do you think we have to renew our mind? Living in a world as we do, I believe renewing our mind is a constant state of being, a mind-set, a lifestyle, because we live in a world that tells us otherwise. Renew your mind constantly by dwelling on God's Word and reminding yourself of who He says you are!

Now, even though our sinful nature has been condemned in the body of Christ, the body and mind can still remember 'bad habits'. This is similar to the phenomena of muscle memory or cellular memory. Muscle memory is the reason we can do something without being conscious of it. I like to think of sinful behavior as a bad habit, or residue, left-over from being born with a sinful nature.

Erasing this "muscle memory" happens when we renew our mind to our new creation in Christ, resulting in our transformation (Romans 12:2). Renewing our mind is when Grace is deposited and received in our heart, naturally producing fruits of righteousness or righteous behavior because we have the nature of Christ. It may take time to show as we are made righteous by learning how to live righteously, but we will bear fruit as we renew our mind and grow in Christ.

If you read Romans 6:2-7, 7:4-6, 8:3-4, 12:2, Galatians 2:20, Ephesians 4:21-24, and Colossians 2:12-13, you can roughly sum them up as:

> *2 Corinthians 5:17 (NIV): Therefore, if anyone is in Christ, he is a new creation; the old has gone, and all has been made new!*

God doesn't resurrect our old, sinful nature to clean it up. He works on our new creation, our new identity in Christ to teach us to live in His wholeness and the finished works of Christ.

Nowhere in the Bible does it say to work on sin. Behavior modification through willpower is not a Biblical doctrine. It is a false teaching of religion. Dying with Christ and being resurrected with Him a new creation, without blemish, is Biblical and is the Gospel of the Grace of Jesus Christ (Colossians 1:22).

Nowhere in the Bible does it say to work on sin. Behavioral modification through willpower is not a Biblical doctrine. It is a false teaching of religion.

Our identity is in Christ who makes all things new. We need to stop referring to ourselves by our dead man and start seeing ourselves as God's new, righteous creation!

God does not deal with our dead man because that is what it is. Dead. God knows we're dead because He watched us die in Christ. God is not watching us under a microscope to see if we've been bad. He already knows we've been bad. Doesn't it make sense that God would take the bad out of us? Our identity is in Christ who makes all things *new*. We need to stop identifying with our old, dead self and start seeing ourselves as God's new, righteous creation in Christ. We have got to believe right to live right.

5.3 A GUILT-FREE CONSCIENCE

Now that we've established salvation, Grace, the law, and God seeing us without blemish, it has undoubtedly caused some questions concerning conviction and confession to arise. Religion has taught us to attribute condemnation as conviction from the Holy Spirit, with the only remedy to confess each and every sin. This cycle leaves us with nothing more than a guilty conscience and an identity as a sinner.

The result is feeling unworthy of being in God's presence because we focus on sin rather than Grace. The problem with this theology is that it leaves us trying to correct our old-dead man who has been condemned and crucified with Christ, rather than focusing on our new creation in Christ who is made righteous, blameless, and without blemish.

> **Sin-consciousness produces a guilty conscience, the very opposite effect of Christ's conscience-cleansing blood.**

We will dig into the Biblical definition of conviction and confession later in the chapter, but we first need to understand why there is a problem in believing conviction and confession are sin-focused. The problem with conviction and confession being sin-focused is that sin-consciousness produces a guilty conscience, the very opposite effect of Christ's conscience-cleansing blood. This sin-focused theology goes against what the blood of Christ has accomplished. Here's why:

> *Romans 7:7-11 (NIV): I would not have known what sin was except through the law. (8) But sin, seizing the opportunity afforded by the commandment, produced in me every kind of covetous desire. For apart from the law, sin is dead.*

In Romans 7:7, we see that it is the law that shows us what sin is and not the Holy Spirit. The law makes us conscious of sin by bringing it to life. And being conscious of sin is a curse. Therefore, when we are feeling condemned or guilty from sin in our life, it is from the enemy (or ourselves) accusing us through the law rather than conviction from the Holy Spirit. We will go deeper into the role of the Holy Spirit later, but we must remember that since the law has been made obsolete, we are now apart from the law (Galatians 3:24-25, Hebrews 8:13).

> *Romans 3:20 (NIV): Therefore, no one will be declared righteous in God's sight by the works of the law; rather, through the law we become conscious of our sin.*

> *Galatians 3:10 (NIV): For all who rely on the works of the law are under a curse.*

The law makes us conscious of sin, producing a guilty conscience through its curse, producing more sin because sin is on the forefront of our consciousness. The blood of Christ cleanses us from this guilty conscience because Christ's blood has paid the price for our sin, washing and cleansing us (Hebrews 9:22), freeing us from the curse of the law so that we may live peacefully in God's presence:

> *Hebrews 9:14 (NIV): How much more, then, will the blood of Christ, who through the eternal Spirit offered himself unblemished to God, cleanse our consciences from acts that lead to death, so that we may serve the living God?*

If you remember back in our discussion on the opposite of Grace, we learned that sin is revived in our life when we are conscious of it and focusing on it will result in its manifestation through behavior. This is a crucial reason why we can't be sin-conscious and why God would never accuse us of being sinners or bring sin to the forefront of our conscience.

> Hebrews 10:19-22 (NIV): *Therefore, brothers, since we have confidence to enter the Most Holy Place by the blood of Jesus, (20) by a new and living way opened for us through the curtain, that is, his body, (21) and since we've a great priest over the house of God, (22) let us draw near to God with a sincere heart in all assurance of faith, having our hearts sprinkled to cleanse us from a guilty conscience and having our bodies washed with pure water.*

THINKING POINT

While obtaining my degree in psychology, I remember reading a study on students who tried to quit swearing. Students were randomly selected and placed in two groups. It was the goal of one group to try and quit swearing and it was the goal of the second group to not. Contrary to what you might think, the group that tried to stop swearing saw a significant increase in their usage of swear words!

This is because swearing was on the forefront of their conscience. And just like being focused on swearing will produce more swearing, focusing on sin, even to try and stop it, will increase in more sinful behavior because it is on the fore-front of our minds. This is the reason it is crucial to focus on Grace and what Christ has accomplished on our behalf on the Cross.

The blood of Christ cleanses our conscience from the curse of a sin-conscience, that leads to death, because it has paid the price for every sin. So, why would God bring sin to our conscience by having conviction and confession focus on sin? Wouldn't this essentially be cursing us? Where in God's Word does Jesus, the Word made flesh (John 1:14), mention the individual sin of another? The closest we can find is the Samaritan woman in John 4:16, but does Jesus really 'call out' her sin?

> John 4:16-18 (NIV): He told her, "Go, call your husband and come back." (17) "I have no husband," she replied. Jesus said to her, "You are right when you say you have no husband. (18) The fact is, you have had five husbands, and the man you now have is not your husband. What you have just said is quite true."

Another example of this was when the Pharisees wanted to stone the adulterous woman. Jesus told them that anyone who was without sin could throw the first stone (John 8:7). Again, Jesus didn't address her sin. He was her advocate.

Jesus was very careful and deliberate in His words. In fact, the only people Jesus 'called out' were the Pharisees and other religious leaders because they were the ones 'calling out' the sin of the people. The Pharisees were perverting the law to condemn and oppress people. Jesus had a very direct, yet compassionate way of addressing sin in the lives of those He touched. He never called out the sin of anyone. He never brought it to the forefront of their consciousness, cursing them. Rather than Jesus condemning people and their sin like many of us believe God does today through conviction, Jesus instructed them to go and leave their sin and live in righteousness.

> John 8:10-11 (NIV): Then Jesus straightened up and asked her, "Woman, where are your accusers? Has no one condemned you?" (11) "No one, Lord," she answered. "Neither do I condemn you," Jesus declared. "Now go and sin no more."

The actions of Jesus are a direct representation of the gentle, compassionate correction we receive in the personal relationship we have with God through the Holy Spirit. And just like Jesus, the Holy Spirit directs our steps into righteousness rather than making us conscious of sin as if we have the power to correct it.

To understand conviction and confession correctly, we must understand that God does not see us as sinners. This is the reason Paul writes that while we *were* sinners (past tense), Christ died for us (Romans 5:8).

In His ultimate wisdom, creativity, and selfless sacrifice of Jesus Christ, God devised and executed a plan to take the 'bad' out of us, that we would be reconciled to Him and His perfect love. This is the relationship God has created for us to have with Him through spilling the blood of Christ. It is a relationship where our conscience is cleansed by His love, freeing us from the bondage of sin. God took the 'bad' out of us through Christ's atonement, also known as the great exchange. To understand conviction and confession properly, we must first understand the great exchange.

THINKING POINT

Do you think you can have the confidence to enter the presence of God while having a guilty conscience? Do you think you can have the confidence to enter the presence of God while being sin-focused?

> Hebrews 4:16 (NIV): Let us then approach God's throne of grace with confidence, so that we may receive mercy and find grace to help us in our time of need.

It is difficult to enter God's presence when we have a guilty conscience from being sin-focused. With sin on our mind, it seems as if God's presence is the last place we feel worthy of being in when, in fact, it's the place we desperately need to be. The reason God tells us to labor to enter His presence (Hebrews 4:11), is because the times we need His presence the most, it's the most difficult to get there because of guilt and shame.

5.4 THE GREAT EXCHANGE

God does not relate to us as sinners because He took the 'bad' out of us. He did this for the very reason of His desire to have a perfect relationship with us through reconciliation. This is the great exchange. Let's understand how God did this.

> Romans 5:11 (NIV): Not only is this so, but we also rejoice in God through our LORD Jesus Christ, through whom we've now received reconciliation.

> Romans 5:11 (KJV): And not only so, but we also joy in God through our LORD Jesus Christ, by whom we've now received the atonement.

As we see in the different translations of Romans 5:11, reconciliation and atonement essentially have similar meanings in God's Word. It is through the act of atonement that we have reconciliation with God, thus having a perfect relationship with Him. We are made righteous or are in 'right standing' with God through the atoning sacrifice, or the reconciliation, of Jesus Christ (Romans 5:2).

Atonement is the core of the great exchange that took place on the Cross and is a powerful word that is not understood by believers today. There are two different "atonements" used in the Bible, a Hebrew form (Old Covenant) and a Greek form (New Covenant). Although they are the same word, relatively, they have vastly different meanings. This confusion is the reason people are still living under the Old Covenant atonement, or the law, and its curse.

The Old Testament or Hebrew word for atonement is "kippur" (כִּפֻּר) and comes from the root word "kaphar" (כָּפַר), and means, "to cover". This covering was only temporary. If you remember, this was the second reason why God created the New Covenant because the Old Covenant only covered sin through the blood of animal sacrifices for a period. It was an annual reminder of sin (Hebrews 10:2-4).

When I think of Old Testament atonement, which means covering, I think back to my childhood when I swept dirt under rugs and shoved toys and dirty laundry under my bed when told to clean my room. My mom began to wonder what was happening when articles of clothing would go missing for extended periods.

To me, this represents the animal sacrifices of the Old Covenant. Despite what is covered, we are still conscious of what is underneath. When we look at the rug, we will be conscious of the dirt underneath, or the dirty clothes under the bed, even though they are out of sight. This is the reason people are still conscious of their sin under the law. They are still living under the Old Covenant, sin-focused, because they believe their sins are only covered, therefore still a part of their identity.

> Hebrews 10:1-4 (NIV): The law is only a shadow of the good things that are coming— not the realities themselves. For this reason it **can never**, by the same sacrifices repeated endlessly year after year, **make perfect** those who draw near to worship. (2) Otherwise, would they not have stopped being offered? For the worshipers would have been cleansed once for all, and would no longer have **felt guilty** for their sins. (3) But those sacrifices are an annual reminder of sins. (4) It is **impossible** for the blood of bulls and goats to take away sins.

The law being a shadow of what was to come (Hebrews 10:1) meant the law was not the reality of what Christ was coming to do. The law was a shadow or representation of what was to take place on the Cross. The law was not God's end-result or final will, so to speak. Note the differences between the Old Covenant compared to the New Covenant:

> The law being a shadow of what was to come meant the law was not the reality of what Christ was coming to do.

1. The animal sacrifices could never make anyone perfect, in contrast to Christ's blood making us perfect (Ephesians 1:4, 5:27, Colossians 1:22).
2. The animal sacrifices could never cleanse us once and for all, in contrast to Christ's blood which does (1 Peter 3:18, Romans 6:10, Hebrews 9:28, Colossians 2:13).
3. It is impossible for the blood of bulls and goats to take away sins, in contrast to the blood of Christ who takes away all sins once and for all (1 Peter 3:18, Romans 6:10, Hebrews 9:28, Colossians 2:13).

In contrast, the New Testament "atonement" in Romans 5:11 is the Greek word "katallagē" (καταλλαγή), and means, "exchange". This definition is to "give up one thing for another, to replace" (dictionary.com). It is not the same as "to cover" (kaphar) in the Old Testament.

In 2 Corinthians 5:21, we see the great exchange or "what was given up for another":

> 2 Corinthians 5:21 (NIV): God made **him who had no sin to be sin** for us, so that in him we might become the **righteousness of God**.

Jesus did not merely cover our sins with His blood as the animals did in the Old Testament. He did infinitely better. He became our sin, exchanging them for His righteousness (2 Corinthians 5:21). This is the great exchange, and because of this exchange, our sins don't exist in God's eyes. In other words, there is no sin to cover anymore because Christ has paid for all of them in full!

If God chose to see our sins, He would have to condemn them in us (death) because He is Holy, just, and perfect. Therefore, Christ would have died in vain. Because our sinful flesh has been condemned and our sins forgiven in our death and resurrection in Christ, when God looks at us He

APPLICATION

Sin does not make you a sinner any more than drinking water makes you a fish. This is the reason Paul was very careful in his words in Romans 5:8: "While we *were* still sinners, Christ died for us."

Don't ever minimize what God has done to make you who you are in Christ today. In your prayers, in how you see yourself, in how you expect to be treated by others, remember who you are in Christ: God's beloved. As you start to see yourself as the righteousness of God through Christ, you will see yourself start to emulate the nature of Christ (1 John 4:17).

sees Christ. This is the reason we are like Christ in this world (1 John 4:17). Christ has replaced our sin with His righteousness. And He has given us the Holy Spirit to empower and lead us to live out His righteousness (Titus 2:12, Philippians 2:13, 2 Corinthians 12:9).

Because of Christ's atonement, sin does not make us a sinner any more than drinking water makes us a fish. God lives in a realm void of time (Psalm 90:4, 139:16, 2 Peter 3:8). He has seen our life from beginning to end, including every sin past, present, and future, placing them on the body of Christ. This is the reason we can live with a cleansed conscience (Hebrews 9:14). There is no sin for God or us to focus on. Christ literally became our sin and we became His righteousness (2 Corinthians 5:21)

5.5 CONVICTION

Now that we understand that being sin-focused is in opposition to what Christ's conscience-cleansing blood accomplished in the great exchange, we can now understand that conviction is meant to remind us of our righteousness rather than sin. This happens through the Holy Spirit. To understand conviction, we need to look at the job description of the Holy Spirit:

> John 16:8-11 (KJV): And when he is come, he will **reprove the world** of sin, and of righteousness, and of judgment: (9) Of sin, because **they** [the world] believe not on me; (10) Of righteousness, because I go to my Father, and ye see me no more; (11) Of judgment, because the prince of this world is judged.

This verse is speaking on the expedience of Jesus ascending to heaven to send us the Holy Spirit (expedient means advantageous or to our advantage), and that the Holy Spirit will reprove the world of sin. In the NIV, the word "convict" is the word used for "reprove". It's interesting that the word "convict" is not found in the King James Version, generally believed to be the most accurate English translation of God's Word. But "reprove" is.

Reprove is the Greek word "elegchō" (ἐλέγχω), and means, "to refute with shame, to bring to the light, or to expose." This refuting with shame is religion's teaching of conviction to the believer, the very shameful and condemning doctrine that man created to induce righteous behavior through fear. This highlighting of sin is to manipulate believers into giving money or serving, for some examples, to get into God's good standing. It is based on man's inferior knowledge and lack of understanding God's perfect love.

> This refuting with shame is religion's teaching of conviction to the believer, the very shameful and condemning doctrine that man created to induce righteous behavior through fear.

In John 16:8, it is important to note who the Holy Spirit is reproving (elegchō): The world. When we take into consideration John 16:9 when Jesus says, "of sin, because *they* believe not in me," He is using "they" in reference to the "world", which is the Greek word "kosmos" (κόσμος), meaning the "the ungodly multitude;

the whole mass of men alienated from God, hostile to the cause of Christ".

It is the job of the Holy Spirit to convict the world of not believing in Jesus. This can be shameful and condemning, and is why the presence of a Spirit-filled believer can put a non-believer on the defense, making them feel uncomfortable while not even directly interacting with one another.

The Holy Spirit brings the darkness to light, exposing the unbelief of the world, and this can be unpleasant. Believers take this verse out of context and think that it is meant for them, thus producing condemnation and guilt when it is referring to those who don't believe in Christ as LORD and Savior. Being we are a new creation in Christ, there is no darkness in us to bring to light because our sinful nature has been condemned in the body of Christ and our sins forgiven.

Does the Holy Spirit use this shameful conviction and condemnation to teach and instruct believers in Christ? To answer this question, we will look at the second job description of the Holy Spirit. In doing so, it's important to remember that the Holy Spirit and the Word of God are synonymous. The Holy Spirit is the Word, and the Word is the Holy Spirit (Hebrews 4:12). Knowing this, we will look to 2 Timothy:

> 2 Timothy 3:16 (KJV): All scripture is given by inspiration of God, and is profitable for doctrine, for reproof, for correction, for instruction in righteousness:

Let us take a look at the Greek translation of 2 Timothy 3:16:
"Doctrine" is "didaskalia" (διδασκαλία): "for teaching or instruction".
"For correction" is "epanorthōsis" (ἐπανόρθωσις): "restoration to an upright or right state", meaning righteousness.
"Instruction" as in "instruction into righteousness," is "paideia" (παιδεία): "the whole training and education of children (which relates to the cultivation of mind and morals) in righteousness".

With that said, the word "reproof" (conviction) in this verse is a different form of "reproof" that is found in John 16:9, as it is the Greek word "elegchos" (ἔλεγχος) and not "elegchō" (ἐλέγχω) as previously exemplified, meaning to refute with shame. This form of conviction, "elegchos", means "a proof, that by which a thing is proved or tested for proof". We find what exactly it proves:

> 2 Corinthians 1:21-22 (NIV): Now it is God who makes both us and you stand firm in Christ. He anointed us, (22) set his seal of ownership on us, and put his Spirit in our hearts as a deposit, guaranteeing what is to come.

The test, or proof, of the Holy Spirit is guaranteeing, or proving, what has been done in us through Christ. The Spirit proves our righteous standing through manifesting in the present, natural realm (Romans 5:2, 2 Corinthians 5:5), taking place when we're Spirit-filled, when God's working in us and through us (Titus 2:12, Philippians 2:13). The evidence of this is the fruits of the Spirit (Galatians 5:22-23), manifested through our ability to love others as Christ loves us (John 13:34, 15:12).

The Holy Spirit is our seal of righteousness, our proof that we have been bought with the blood of Jesus. He is our deposit that we receive from choosing God in this life while having free will, becoming our down payment, guaranteeing salvation and preservation throughout eternity. Using our free will to choose God over evil in this

> Conviction is God reminding us of how He sees us when what we do is not aligned with who we are in Christ.

realm solidifies our free will through eternity in the Heavenly realm, where evil does not exist. This is one reason we must live in a realm where evil is a choice.

If you remember, "preserved" is one of the definitions of salvation. The Holy Spirit is our proof of the preservation of our righteous standing in Christ until His second-coming. It is proof that the law is fulfilled through living a Holy Spirit directed life; proof that we can love others as God loves us (John 15:12).

Conviction is God instructing us into righteousness when what we do isn't aligned with who we are in Christ. It is God reminding us that we are without blemish, that our righteous standing in Christ is permanent (Romans 5:2).

As we saw in 2 Timothy 3:16, the Word of God and the Holy Spirit teaches us (didaskalia), instructs us into righteousness (paideia), and corrects us to an upright or right state (epanorthōsis), thus proving (elegchos) who we are in Christ by showing and empowering us to live as Christ lived (John 14:12, 1 John 4:17).

APPLICATION

When God corrects us through conviction, it may not always feel pleasant. I believe this is the reason why it is so easy for us to attach condemnation and guilt to conviction.

The more we fall in love with God, the more our heart will sink when we know we are not living up to His expectations for us, which is to be Christ-like (1 John 4:17). I experience the same response when I hurt my wife or let her down, even though it was not my intent. I love her so much that knowing I did not perform to the best of my ability, through Christ, I feel sorrow. This sorrow is a good remorse as it leads to reconciliation and repentance, but never let it turn into condemnation, guilt, or shame.

In all we have discussed, I see nothing of the sort that God uses shameful conviction (elegchō) to guide, teach, and direct believers with shameful reproof or bringing darkness to the light. We are children of the light. We cannot be a child of darkness and a child of the light at the same time. Two opposing realities cannot exist in the same domain. Light can't exist in darkness and darkness can't exist in light. We are in Christ and we are the light unto the world (Matthew 5:14), and this is how God sees us.

> Rather than God reminding us of everything we do wrong, He shows us through his Word and Holy Spirit who we are and how He has empowered us to live.

Anytime "elegchō" is used in the context of producing guilt or shame, it is used in reference to unbelievers. Thus, anytime we experience condemnation, guilt, or shame, it is not from God (Romans 1:16) and we are listening to a lie from the accuser (Revelation 12:10). Instead of God reminding us of everything we do wrong, He shows us through His Word and Holy Spirit who we are and how He has empowered us to live. Remember, upon salvation we're made whole. Life is learning how to live in God's wholeness.

THINKING POINT

The Self-Fulfilling Prophecy is a study of a phenomenon known concerning children in school. What this study found is that children who are taught by a teacher who has low expectations for them will regress and perform to those low expectations. In contrast, children who are taught by teachers who have high expectations of them will perform up to those expectations.

Since God created science, children, and how they learn, we know this principle applies to our relationship with Him. God has high expectations of us and part of the reason we stay in bondage to sin is that we think God is always condemning us or relating to us as sinners. We confuse conviction for condemnation because we don't know any better, and then wonder why we stay regressed in sin and distant from God, even becoming angry and bitter towards Him.

Conviction is an identity correction, not a behavioral correction. However, Gods instruction and teaching into righteousness results in a behavioral correction through reminding us (renewing of the mind) who we are in Christ (identity). Religion has taught us to receive the lies of the enemy, bringing shame and condemnation by attributing it as conviction from the Holy Spirt. In fact, oftentimes condemnation is not even from the enemy. We do such a 'bang-up' job of condemning ourselves by rejecting the ability to relate to God and receive His forgiveness when we mess-up.

We have been taught by religion to accuse and condemn ourselves and one another. We as a church, as in the body of Christ, really do not believe that our sins have been paid in full, and we condemn ourselves when we fall short, producing a guilty conscience. We then wonder why we can't break the bondage of sin. We can't break the bondage of sin in our life when we don't believe God has made us a new creation in Christ.

> God proving or reminding us that we are His righteousness through Christ is infinitely more productive than bringing up our sin that has already been paid for by the blood of Christ.

God proving or reminding us that we are His righteousness through Christ is infinitely more productive than bringing up sin that has already been paid for by the blood of Christ. God does not raise our dead man to correct him into righteousness. He teaches and instructs our new creation in Christ to live righteously. Grace empowers us to live as God sees us—righteous in Christ.

God has high expectations of us. He is constantly reminding us of our righteous standing in Christ and that we have been empowered to live as Christ in this world (John 14:12, Romans 5:2, 1 John 4:17).

5.6 CONFESSION

Now in continuing our train of thought, if Christ became our sin in exchange for His righteousness and God has forgiven us of all sins, why are we told to confess them?

Biblical confession is meant to receive salvation. And rather than confession reinforcing a false identity as a sinner, confession is meant to disassociate ourselves from sin through reminding ourselves of who we are in Christ. We will first look to 1 John 1:9:

> **Rather than confession reinforcing a false identity as a sinner, confession is meant to disassociate ourselves from sin through reminding ourselves of who we are in Christ.**

> *1 John 1:9 (KJV): If we confess our sins, he is faithful and just to forgive us our sins, and to cleanse us from all unrighteousness.*

APPLICATION

How powerful do you think it is when you confess the same thing that God says about who you are?

Romans 10:9 (NKJV): that if you confess with your mouth the LORD Jesus and believe in your heart that God has raised Him from the dead, you will be saved.

In Romans 10:9, what came before believing? Confession! If you have difficulty believing your worth in Christ, confess that you are the righteousness of God in Christ and you just watch your beliefs take form and change the way you see yourself!

If Jesus paid for sins once and for all, and all our sins have been forgiven, past, present, and future (Hebrews 10:10,12, Colossians 2:13), what is 1 John 1:9 speaking of?

The word used for "sins" in 1 John 1:9, as in "if we confess our sins", is the Greek word "hamartia" (ἁμαρτία). This word means: "to be without a share in; to miss the mark". However, it is a negative particle meaning it is making a statement or fact about one's existing state. This makes it singular and not plural. This is a big deal because "sins" in 1 John 1:9, in its original Greek form, is singular as in "sin", not plural as in "sins" we commit.

To help us understand a little more, in Vine's Expository Dictionary the Greek word "hamartia" for "sins" is referring to "a principle or source of action, or an inward element producing acts".

When we take these two definitions of "harmartia" into account, 1 John 1:9 is referring to where "sins" originate from, which is our sinful flesh. This confession is in the context of salvation, asking for forgiveness of all our trespasses, asking God to cleanse us from "all unrighteousness". We are confessing our need for a Savior, leading to salvation.

In 1 John 1, John is introducing Jesus as the incarnation of the Word of God to unbelievers, telling them salvation comes through the confession of their sins or their sinful nature, proclaiming that Jesus Christ is LORD and Savior.

When speaking of where sins originate from, it's important to understand the condition in which we were born. Most people believe that we are born in the image of God when we were born into this world. How can we be born in the image of God when we are born in sinful flesh or with a sinful nature? God is perfect. He has neither of those conditions in Him. We can't be both born in God's image and in sin.

Adam was born in the image of God. When he sinned the image he was born into, his God-like image, died. Thus, his sons (including us) were born of his image, or of the sinful nature, which is what we are told to confess in 1 John 1:9. We see that humankind is born in Adam's image, in his fallen nature, in Genesis 5:

> Genesis 5:3 (NIV): When Adam had lived 130 years, he had a son in his own likeness, in his own image; and he named him Seth.

The truth is, we are not born in the image of God until we are saved, born again, crucified, and resurrected with Jesus Christ.

Now, back to confession. The word "confess" is the Greek word "homologeō" (ὁμολογέω), and means, "to say the same thing as another, i.e. to agree with, assent, to concede". Confession means to say the same thing as God or His Word; to agree with what He says.

Confessing Jesus Christ as LORD brings salvation. Our continuing transformation happens by the renewing of our mind (Romans 12:2), which takes place by confessing the same thing as what God says about us in His Gospel of Grace. And if you remember, the Gospel of Grace says that we are perfect and blameless, the righteousness of God in Christ. This changes our perception of ourselves as sinners and reinforces our identity as a new creation; a child of God.

And His Word, His very Gospel of Grace says that we are without blemish (Colossians 1:22). God relates to us as He sees us and if we continue saying the same thing as God's Word says about ourselves, we will start to live as He has created and empowered us to live: As Christ-like (1 John 4:17).

APPLICATION

Confessing our faults to one another is imperative to conquer sin in our life. We have got to have godly people in our lives for support, to encourage us and to speak God's truth into our lives during the times we need it the most.

Think about 2 or 3 people who you know that would be willing to be your accountability partner. They need to be people who are grounded in God's Word and living in His love every day. They will be individuals that you can trust and count on, those who will pray with you and for you, and speak God's Word into your life. And when the time is right, you will fulfill that role in the life of another.

The words that we speak over ourselves and others are powerful, whether positive or negative. We see the power of our words in James:

> *James 3:2 (KJV): For in many things we offend all. If any man offend not in word, the same is a perfect man, and able to also bridle the whole body.*

The degree of control we have over our tongue is the degree of control we will have over our body, therefore behavior. When we use the power of our tongue and say the same thing as God says about who we are, it will control our body to live out what we are confessing: Our righteousness in Christ!

THINKING POINT

What if you had a friend who pointed out everything you did wrong in life? How long would it take before you began to resent that friend, tried to avoid them, or even finally stopped speaking to them?

Why do we think our relationship with the Holy Spirit, our Comforter, is any different? How is comfort derived from being sin-conscious or having sin thrown into our face? This doctrine and understanding of man does not make sense in the realm of Grace.

James 5 has another verse on confession that can provoke confusion when not understood. Notice the difference in translations of James 5:16:

> *James 5:16 (NIV): Therefore confess your sins to each other and pray for each other so that you may be healed.*

> *James 5:16 (KJV): Confess your faults one to another, and pray one for another, that ye may be healed.*

This "confess" in James 5:16 is a different form of the word "confess" that we previously discussed, as it is the Greek word *"exomologeō"* (ἐξομολογέω), not "homologeō" (ὁμολογέω). *"Exomologeō"* means to *profess*, specifically, "to profess that one will do something, to promise, to agree".

First, notice who we're confessing to: One another! God already knows our sin and has wiped them away with the blood of Christ. This doesn't mean there is no value in confessing to God. But it has to be done in the context of acknowledging our righteousness in Christ. In doing so, we take hold of our empowerment through grace.

Second, the word "sins" in James 5:16 is more accurately translated as "faults," and is the Greek word "paraptōma" (παράπτωμα), and means, "a lapse or deviation from truth and uprightness". When we are told to "confess our sins" in James 5:16, or more accurately "profess our faults", we are professing or *claiming our authority* or empowerment through the Holy Spirit over the struggles we are facing. We are acknowledging the victory we have in Christ over the sins we are struggling with. This is accountability.

When we profess, we are speaking our beliefs into existence making our faith effectual (Philemon 1:6). We are to profess not only our sins or faults to our friends, asking for accountability, but also our authority in Christ over them. We have power and authority over the sin in our life. Sometimes we don't feel like it when sin can be over-whelming and we go back to an identity as a sinner living in condemnation, guilt, and shame.

When you combine the power of our beliefs and add the power of life or death in the tongue (Proverbs 18:21), we can understand the power in professing our victory in Christ over the bondages of sin in our life.

Confession, or professing, is not asking God to give us strength to overcome. Professing *proclaims* that we *will* change our behavior because we are the righteousness of God in Christ. Our body and behavior will follow (James 3:2).

Sin thrives in secrecy. When we keep our troubles in secret they will thrive and control us. When we expose sin, especially fear and doubt, to the light through accountability with those we trust, it becomes exposed and then destroyed.

Sin thrives in secrecy. When we keep our troubles in secret they will thrive and have control over us.

Acknowledging the depth of God's love for us and what He accomplished through Christ will have an infinitely greater effect on conquering sin in our life, rather than empowering sin through being conscious or focusing on it.

When we confess, we speak the same thing as God or His gospel about our sinful nature. We acknowledge that God has condemned our sinful nature in the body of Christ, that it is not who we are (identity), and that we are the righteousness of God through Jesus Christ. When we profess, we acknowledge our empowerment and authority, through the Holy Spirit, over the sin in our life with those we trust.

Sin is empowered when we dwell in a guilty conscience, believing we are a sinner. Conviction and confession are meant to remind ourselves that we're not a sinner, that Christ became our sin in exchange for His righteousness. We remind ourselves of how God sees us--that we are His righteousness through Christ.

Acknowledging the depth of God's love for us and what He accomplished through Christ will have an infinitely greater effect on conquering sin in our life, rather than empowering sin through being conscious or focusing on it, cursing ourselves, leading to condemnation, guilt, and shame.

The place where Grace super-abounds over sin is in our heart. When we are Grace-conscious rather than sin-conscious, we are reminded of God's perfect love for us rather than believing we need to be 'good enough' or 'worthy' enough to earn His love. Knowing that we are freely justified and loved is how Grace cleanses our conscience, purifying our heart, empowering us through the Holy Spirit to conquer sin in our life. We are empowered to live as how God sees us. This is when God's nature becomes ours, and sin is not in our nature. This is the truth that sets us free (John 8:32). Remember, it is God who strengthens us to overcome our sin (Titus 2:12; Philippians 2:13, 2 Corinthians 12:9), not us. This is the power of Grace.

THINKING POINT

Some live under a 'works' mentality by believing they have to confess each and every sin in their life for God to forgive them. If our salvation, or even righteous standing, were based on our confession of each and every sin, our perfect standing in Christ would be mediated by our ability and not Christ's. This would not be grace because it would be based on our ability to keep our righteousness through confession rather than the perfect ability of Christ (Hebrews 9:15).

If repentance was based on our confession of every sin, being God is perfect, if we forgot to confess one single sin, we would lose our righteousness in Christ. How sure are you that you would be able to confess each and every sin, not forgetting any? Under this 'works' theology, we would have to confess every sin because repentance, changing one's mind, would not happen through confessing all our sins at once. How can we repent and change our behavior for a sin that we don't even remember committing? I know I can't remember all of them!

Confession is not sin-focused, but rather speaking the same thing as God says about us in His gospel of grace: That we are made a new creation, perfect and spotless in Christ. YOU are the righteousness of God (2 Corinthians 5:21)!

INDIVIDUAL/GROUP DISCUSSION QUESTIONS

1. Why is it important to understand that the law is not meant to guide our living; that focusing on it is a 'problem'? (Galatians 5:4, Romans 8:3-4)

_____

_____

_____

_____

2. How does the blood of Christ affect our conscience, and how? (Hebrews 9:14, 10:19-22; p.66)

_____

_____

_____

_____

3. What has taken place that God does not see the 'bad' in us, but sees us without blemish, faultless, and blameless? (Romans 8:3-4; p.68-69)

_____

_____

_____

_____

4. In your own words, explain the difference between the Old Testament and New Testament definitions for "atonement." What was the problem with the Old Covenant "atonement"? (Hebrews 10:3-4; p.68-69)

_____

_____

_____

_____

5. Why is it important to realize that Holy Spirit conviction is reminding us of who we are in Christ rather than reminding us that we are a sinner? (Galatians 3:10, 13, Hebrews 9:14, 10:22; p.73)

_____

_____

_____

_____

6. What is the Biblical definition of confession? (p.75)

_____

_____

_____

_____

7. Who does God say we are in His Gospel of Grace? (Colossians 1:22-23)

_____

_____

_____

_____

CHAPTER 6

FAITH: PUTTING BELIEFS INTO ACTION

6.1 FAITH UNVEILED

Our discussion on beliefs has included the power of beliefs in that they determine what is fact or "how things are" in our life, that inaccurate beliefs produce a barrier between God and us because we can't worship what we don't believe in, and we have established beliefs of truth in the loving nature and character of God. Now we need to understand the difference between beliefs and faith.

> When people are frustrated with their walk with God, it is because they lack faith, which is derived from hope and rooted in the knowledge of God and His perfect love.

When asked what the difference is between beliefs and faith, most do not know. It can be hard to differentiate between the two. Some even think they are the same. When people are frustrated with their walk with God, it is because they lack faith, which is derived from hope and rooted in the knowledge of God and His perfect love. On the surface they may think they have faith, when in reality they only have beliefs, and most often inaccurate beliefs. This is a reason why we can lack seeing the results of faith in life or the lives of others.

Hebrews gives the definition of faith in Chapter 11:

> Hebrews 11:1 (KJV): Now faith is the substance of things hoped for, the evidence of things not seen.

Most understand faith as believing in something they do not see, such as the wind. Although partially correct as we see from Hebrews, they skip the first half of this verse and end up with only half the definition of faith. They miss the most important component of faith, which is hope. When we take half the definition and leave our concept of faith as only believing in what we do not see, or "the evidence of things not seen", it is not faith but a simple belief, such as believing the wind exists without the hope of harnessing its power to fly a kite. Let's read this verse again:

> Hebrews 11:1 (KJV): Now faith is the substance of things hoped for, the evidence of things not seen.

The Greek word for "substance" is "hypostasis" (ὑπόστασις), and means, "that which has actual existence; a substance, real being".

Most people believe that faith is believing in what one does not or cannot see. However, there is a tangibility and substance to faith; an actual existence that can be seen and measured. So, how can we measure faith?

Hope is a component of faith that most don't realize, and it is this hope that is tangibly seen in behavior, therefore reality. In other words, hope-based behavior is the substance, or tangibility, of faith that can be seen and measured.

> *James 2:14 (KJV): What doth it profit, my brethren, though a man say he hath faith, and have not works? Can faith save him?*

Hope is a component of faith and is tangibly seen in behavior, therefore reality. In other words, hope-based behavior is the substance of faith.

> *James 2:17 (KJV): Even so faith, if it hath not works, is dead, being alone.*

In James 2:14, we see a different "works" than the 'works' mentality we discussed as being so detrimental when under the law (Romans 3:28). Faith "works" are natural fruits of righteousness that manifest in behavior (Galatians 5:22-23). This hope-based behavior is a result of a confident expectation of God's goodness and experiencing His perfect love. This is the polar-opposite of the 'works' done under the law to try and earn a righteous standing with God through our own ability.

The key to giving faith substance is by having a decision-making process (or thought process) based on hope. Faith gains substance when we make decisions with a confident expectation of God's goodness in life.

The tangibility of faith is the result of placing our beliefs of hope into action. If all we have is a belief in God, even accurate beliefs, but no faith, we will go nowhere because our beliefs will just stagnate in our mind. So, how do we put our beliefs into action? How do we make faith evident or tangible in life? How do we give faith substance?

The key to giving faith substance in life is by having a decision-making process (or thought process) established in hope. Faith gains substance when we make decisions with a confident expectation of God's goodness in life.

If all we have is a belief in God, even accurate beliefs, but no faith, we will go nowhere because our beliefs will just stagnate in our mind.

There is a drastic difference between making decisions based on fear and making decisions based on hope in that we are confident that God will do what He has promised in His Word. The difference between hope and fear is the difference between truth and life, and death.

When we make decisions based on fear, science shows that the reasoning and judgment portion of our brain is not included or is overridden by our fear circuits. This is the reason why decisions made in fear are the ones we end up regretting, causing us to look back and think, "What was I thinking!"

The reality is that we were not thinking as God created us to think because fear overrode our thought process. This is what the Bible calls a "reprobate mind" (Romans 1:28): A mind not functioning wholly or as it should.

THINKING POINT

This might take some reflection but think about a time when you made a decision that you regretted. Can you remember your motives for making that decision? Were your motives based on the peace, security, and stability of God's perfect love, knowing He will do what His Word has promised you? Or were your motives based on fear, specifically, fear or insecurity that you would go without, or lack something in your life? Fear is based on unbelief, and unbelief is based on not believing God is faithful; that He won't do what He has promised us in His Word.

In contrast, when we make decisions while saturated with God's peace and love, our fear circuits shut down allowing us to make decisions based on the part of our brain that we use for reason and logic (prefrontal cortex), giving us better judgment. A fully functioning mind absent of the presence of fear is what the Bible calls a "sound mind" (2 Timothy 1:7). The works or fruit of our faith are tangibly seen when decisions are made in God's presence, experiencing the fullness of His love daily.

Faith-based hope that guides behavior is a certainty that God will do what He has promised us in His Word, thus, decisions will not be made out of the fear of lack, but rather, in the confidence and security of God's perfect love. The natural product of our hope-based decisions will be fruits of righteous behaviors (Isaiah 32:17, Galatians 5:22-23, Philippians 1:11).

When we live life with a confident expectation of God's goodness, we will not enter in to dysfunctional relationships, for example, because we are secure in God's love, confident He will bring us the right person at the right time. We will also be generous in giving to those in need because we have a confident expectation that God will provide us more of what He already has given us.

6.2 GREAT FAITH

When speaking of faith, there are two individuals in the Bible who Jesus described as having "great faith": A Roman centurion (Luke 7:1-10) and a house-wife (Mathew 15:21-28). When we hear of having "great faith", what do you think it means? And how do we get it?

One of the things I've found in studying God's Word is that it compares and contrasts beautifully between events or themes. When we look at the centurion and the house-wife, the only thing they have in common is their "great faith". When we contrast them, they could not be more opposite from one another. If you were to compare and contrast the characteristics of the centurion and the house-wife, what would be some of the similarities, as well as differences, between the two?

The only common denominator between the Roman centurion and the house-wife, other than faith, is that they were Gentiles or non-Jews. This means they were

> The only common denominator between the Roman centurion and the house-wife is that they were Gentiles, or non-Jews. This means they were unaware of sin or not (sin-)conscious from living under the law of Moses.

unaware of sin, or not (sin-)conscious from living under the Law of Moses. And remember, the law is the opposite of Grace.

Back in the time of Jesus under the Old Covenant, the ability of the Jews to be blessed by God hinged on their obedience to the law or 'works' (following the law perfectly and performing sin offerings). In contrast, Gentiles (non-Jews) knew nothing of living under the law as it was not ingrained in their culture.

The reason their lack in knowledge of the law was empowering is because the opposite of faith is not fear or disbelief, but the law. The centurion and house-wife were able to believe in Grace because they were not under the law, thus they were able to exhibit not only faith, but great faith. Righteousness is through faith, not obedience to the law (Romans 3:22).

> Romans 3:28 (NIV): For we maintain that a person is justified by faith apart from the works of the law.

In understanding how the law inhibits faith, it is critical to understand that the law was given to make us conscious of sin, therefore a curse, and nothing more (Romans 3:20). In fact, there is nothing more it can do.

It is impossible to achieve justification and righteousness through obedience to the law, as Paul states: "Therefore, no one will be declared righteous in His sight by observing the law" (Romans 3:20).

APPLICATION

When you are conscious of your state because of the law, you fail to see your perfect, righteous standing in Christ (Romans 5:2). Your focus is fixed on yourself rather than what Christ has accomplished for you on the Cross.

Our tendency to focus on ourselves or our circumstances is why God's Word tells us to seek Him first, that all things will be added unto us (Matthew 6:33)! When we place more focus on God than ourselves, we will be amazed at the direction we will receive, the perception we will have, along with His peace, wisdom, and discernment in making life's decisions.

What you focus on is what you will live in.

For Jews, the law was central to their families, culture and traditions, much like 'works', being good enough or doing enough good things are central to religion. The Jews had to uphold the law to have a relationship with God along with the covering of their sins through animal sacrifices.

In Romans 3:21, Paul writes that we achieve righteousness through faith in Jesus Christ and not by deeds or 'works'. In reality, the law condemns and curses those who rely on it (2 Corinthians 3:6-9, Galatians 3:10).

When we are conscious of our state because of the law, we fail to see our perfect, righteous standing in Christ (Romans 5:2). This happens when our focus is on ourselves or our temporary state, rather than our perfect, righteous standing in Christ. This is easy for us to do because we tend to only focus on what we can see:

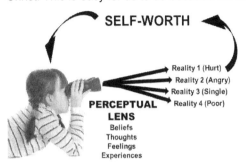

Our imperfect, natural, temporary state. Our temporary state is governed by our physical, emotional, and mental feelings and thoughts. They change with time and can change at any moment. They impact our perception of reality, therefore reality itself and, as we discussed in Week 1, our self-worth.

Our standing, on the other hand, is permanent and does not change (Romans 5:2). It is important to understand that this is the realm of faith. Our faith leads us through the Holy Spirit, not the law, into an everlasting standing throughout eternity (Romans 8:4).

We need to remember to judge ourselves by our state, making adjustments accordingly to the Holy Spirit's direction, and measure ourselves by our perfect, righteous standing in Christ (Romans 5:2).

Our state and standing are the difference between the law and Grace. The law shows us our imperfect state, while Grace shows us our perfect, righteous standing in Christ.

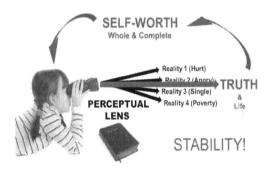

2 Corinthians 3:18 (KJV): But we all, with open face beholding as in a glass the glory of the LORD, are changed into the same image from glory to glory, even as by the Spirit of the LORD.

6.3 FAITH PURIFIES THE HEART

Because of Grace, we are given the nature of Christ through our belief and faith in Him. Through faith, Christ is in us and we are in Him (1 John 4:13). This makes faith an enabler through Christ's finished works, for us to be transformed into the image of Christ (Acts 15:8-9, 2 Corinthians 3:18), to be empowered by the Holy Spirit to live as Christ lived (John 14:12). The result of living life in faith through grace and not 'works', is that it purifies our heart through living a Holy Spirit-influenced life.

> **Knowing God through His Spirit will lead to a purified heart because the only substance that will entice us, that we will crave, will be more of His presence.**

A pure heart is a heart that does not gratify the sinful nature. Our sinful nature has been crucified with Christ (Romans 6:5-7). Therefore, the bondage of sin has been broken through the power of Grace, resulting in our lacking the desires of the sinful flesh (Galatians 5:16) because we have something greater inside of us: God's perfect and fulfilling love.

I guarantee you that the more we get to know God, the less and less enticing sin will be in our life. Knowing God through His Spirit will lead to a purified heart because the only substance that will entice us, that we will crave, will be more of His presence.

THINKING POINT

Did you know that gold is a pure element because it is made of a single element: Gold.

In the same way, a pure heart is only made up of one motive: To know God. A pure heart is a heart that is only after God's will and nothing more, and you have to know Him to know His will. This is awesome because the more you get to know God, the more that knowing you are simply pleasing Him will be the most gratifying feeling on the planet! All the blessings and provision that follow are just a bonus.

The place where Grace overpowers sin is in our heart. Grace overpowers sin when we are living a Holy Spirit-influenced life, thus fulfilling the law (Romans 8:4). Remember, faith without action is dead (James 2:14-17). Action results from beliefs that we have in Christ and manifests or is placed into action through behaviors motivated by a willingness to let the Holy Spirit empower and direct our life.

Let's see how this works! Let's understand the process of how Grace overpowers sin in our heart.

> *1 John 3:19-21 (NIV): This then is how we know that we belong to the truth, and how we set our hearts at rest in his presence (20) whenever our hearts condemn us. For God is greater than our hearts, and He knows everything. (21) Beloved, if our heart condemns us not, then we have confidence toward God.*

We cannot confidently enter the presence of God when we have a condemning heart. It's in these times of condemnation, guilt, and shame that we need to place our faith-based hope in the blood of Christ. It's the blood of Christ that has purified us to be worthy of entering God's presence with confidence, allowing us to be at rest in His perfect love. This understanding is crucial in times of experiencing condemnation, guilt, and shame because it is in His presence that we experience His path of life, the fullness of His joy and pleasures forevermore (Psalm 16:11).

REAL LIFE

Before Justin's transformation, he struggled with sexual promiscuity and would have one-night stands with women he didn't know. There was a time when Justin tried to quit this lifestyle because of how destructive and dangerous it was becoming. After being with a woman, he would make a vow the next morning that this was the end of it. However, the change did not take place at the heart-level. So, the next time Justin received a call, or an opportunity presented itself, Justin took it. He was self-medicating for living a life tormented by hurts and regrets. His self-medication was sex and alcohol.

Thankfully, transformation did take place. God changed Justin's heart and repentance truly happened. Justin's heart was healed and made whole, therefore his mind and decision-making processes changed to align with God's nature. An example of this was after Justin's supernatural transformation, he was working at a moving company. While moving a client, Justin removed his sweatpants, with shorts underneath, because he was getting overheated. At that time, the woman he was moving walked around the corner and grinned, making a very sexually charged statement.

Before Justin was healed, he would have taken this opportunity to capitalize on the woman's statement, asking for her number, inviting her to dinner knowing where it would lead. But that was not Justin's nature anymore. Rather than seeing a woman as an opportunity to temporarily and selfishly fix an addiction, his heart was grieved. He literally felt her pain and suffering from a recent divorce, seeing her need for the love of Jesus to heal and restore her heart. God had given Justin such joy and fulfillment in that he had no desire for that fleshy and carnal indulgence despite gratifying in those experiences for years.

Grace overpowered sin in Justin's heart. God's nature and passions became his, purifying his heart in that the only desire Justin craves, is more of God's perfect love and presence (Titus 2:12, Philippians 2:13, 2 Corinthians 12:9).

When we let condemnation, guilt, and shame dwell in us, when we live in it, is when we make decisions based on fear rather than in the peace and stability of God's perfect love. Decisions made in fear and those made in the peace and love of God's presence will lead to drastically different results. If we do not have faith in Christ's blood, we cannot have confidence, therefore we cannot have peace, nor joy, healing, pleasures, fulfillment, fullness, completeness, etc.

To sum this up:

1. If we experience condemnation, we will not have faith-based hope, therefore we cannot have peace.
2. If we do not have faith-based hope, we cannot have confidence, therefore we cannot have peace.

Peace is crucial because it is the precursor to direction, joy, healing, fulfillment, completeness, and the fullness of God; all being fruits of hope (faith) because we are confident that God will do what His Word promises.

We will have peace if we have confidence in what Christ accomplished on the Cross. If we have peace then we are on our way to stability, because it is in God's peace that we hear His voice of direction for our life. Without peace, how can we hear the still, small, voice of God amongst the loud circumstances of everyday life?

Romans 5:1-2 (NIV): Therefore, having been justified by faith, we have peace with God through our LORD Jesus Christ, (2) through whom also we have obtained our introduction by faith into this grace in which we stand; and we exult in hope of the glory of God.

> **Without peace, how can we hear the still, small, voice of God amongst the loud circumstances of everyday life?**

John 14:24 (NIV): Peace I leave with you; my peace I give you. I do not give to you as the world gives. Do not let your hearts be troubled and do not be afraid.

Without faith, it is impossible to please God (Hebrews 11:6). In other words, without confidence in what Christ accomplished on the Cross, we cannot please God because He desires us to live in His peace, direction, and empowerment. Without confidence, we cannot make decisions in the peace and joy of the LORD, which is our strength (Nehemiah 8:10). We cannot be a cheerful giver if we give with no confidence in God to supply our needs. We cannot experience forgiveness if we are not confident in God's act of already forgiving us. We can't make healthy decisions in relationships if we are not confident in God *alone* to fulfill our needs.

Here is why confidence is so important:

Ephesians 3:12 (NIV): In him and through faith in him we may approach God with freedom and confidence.

1 John 3:19-21 (NIV): This then is how we know that we belong to the truth, and how we set our hearts at rest in his presence (20) whenever our hearts condemn us.

Condemnation will keep us from boldly entering God's presence, or His rest. And it is in His presence where we receive our inheritances of salvation in life

APPLICATION

Confidence is a critical word in the scripture because with confidence in God's Word, you can't help but believe you will see all His promises fulfilled in your life (Isaiah 55:11). From this same place of confidence comes the ability to enter God's presence and rest, where His direction to guide you into His promises takes place.

> Condemnation will keep us from boldly entering God's presence. And it is in His presence that we receive our inheritances of salvation in life.

Psalm 16:11 (KJV): Thou wilt show me the path of life: in thy presence is fullness of joy; at thy right hand there are pleasures for evermore.

Remember, faith puts our beliefs into action through our decision-making process. We have been designed and created to make decisions in God's presence and rest, in His peace. We were not created to carry our cares. Carrying our cares leads to stress, anxiety, and then fear followed by unbelief.

1 Peter 5:7 (KJV): Casting all your care upon him; for he careth for you.

All sin is rooted in unbelief. Sin results when one does not believe that God will do what He has promised in His Word. The result is decisions made in fear, a fear of 'lacking', rather than decisions made in hope with a confident expectation of God's goodness and provision.

> Remember, faith puts our beliefs into action through our decision-making process.

When we are confident in God's ability and desire to do what His Word has promised us, decisions will be made in peace and confidence resulting in behaviors that are based on God's peace and love that passes understanding (Ephesians 3:19, Philippians 4:7).

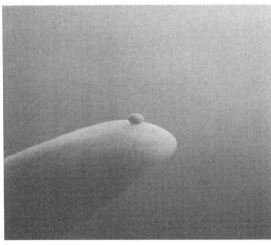

Now that we understand what faith is and that it enables us to make decisions with a confident expectation of God's goodness, let us understand a common misconception about the size of one's faith.

The reason the mustard seed is used as an analogy for the size of faith, is that the size of our faith is irrelevant. We either have faith or we do not. Noah either decided to build the ark or he didn't. We either choose to harness the wind and fly a kite or we don't. It is not the size of our faith; it's whether we have it or not.

One of the most detrimental things we can say to a believer in turmoil is: "You just need more faith." Reality is, they don't have faith. They lack the knowledge (2 Peter 1:3) of hope and confidence in God's ability and love. In telling them, "You need more faith", we are enabling them to continue to dwell in their state of hopelessness rather than teaching them how to have hope through a confident expectation of God's goodness. We need to encourage them to have faith in God's ability and love for them for the current circumstances in their life.

When the Bible talks about "increasing in faith" or when it says, "their faith grew", it is speaking of applying faith to more areas of life; into more decision-making processes of everyday reality. We were created to make decisions in the presence of God, in a state of peace, joy, and with the fullness of God (Psalm 16:11, Ephesians 3:19) where nothing is missing and nothing is lacking (1 Samuel 30:19).

> *2 Corinthians 2:4-5 (NIV): And my speech and my preaching was not with enticing words of man's wisdom, but in demonstration of the Spirit and of power: (5) That your faith should not stand in the wisdom of men, but in the power of God.*

"Demonstration of the Spirit and of power" in 2 Corinthians 2:4 happens through faith manifesting the substance of hope, which are behaviors resulting from decisions made with the confident expectation of God's goodness, resulting in fruits of righteousness (Galatians 5:22-23).

THINKING POINT

Do you make decisions in your life based in confidence knowing God will do what His Word has promised you? If we made decisions based on the peace and love of God, would we make decisions to enter dysfunctional relationships? Would we buy new shoes, a watch, or an outfit, leading to credit card debt to make us feel better about ourselves? Would we resort to addictions to seemingly receive instant gratification over anxiety and stress, or to dull fear? In all these circumstances we find ourselves in, know that God's Word says He will give us the desires of our heart (Psalm 37:4, Matthew 6:33)! But it is only the desires of a pure heart that we have in seeking Him first!

Think about some decisions of the past. Did you make them in God's presence, with confidence knowing He will do what He has promised? Or have you been motivated by the outcome of your decisions rather than being motivated by a desire to fulfill God's purpose for your life?

6.4 NOAH'S FAITH

There are two important reasons why we are going to learn about Noah's "great faith." The first reason being, if we're going to learn about our identity in Christ through the perfect love of God and His goodness, we're going to have to address stories in the Bible, such as the flood, that cause many to question God's perfect love. The second reason is to help us understand what kind of world Noah lived in so we can understand the magnitude of both Noah's faith and God's perfect love for humankind.

Genesis 6:9 (KJV): These are the generations of Noah: Noah was a just man and perfect in his generation, and Noah walked with God.

The Hebrew phrase for "These are the generations of Noah," is "towlĕdah" (תּוֹלְדֹת), and means, "a genealogical list of one's descendants". The context of this verse is Noah's lineage and is pretty straight forward.

The next time the word "generations" is used in the same verse, it is a different Hebrew word, the word "dowr" (דּוֹר), meaning "a period, generation, habitation, or dwelling". It is referring to the period when Noah lived.

Now that we understand the context of Genesis 6:9, what do we think it means when it says Noah was perfect in his "dowr" or "time period"? When it says that Noah was perfect among his generation, I would argue that according to the context of this verse, when it calls Noah "perfect", it is referring to his perfection being of a genetically pure human heredity or genealogy. I know this sounds crazy! But bear with me. As always, we will look to God's Word.

If we look at the translation of Genesis 6:9 by Dr. E. W. Bullinger, a well-recognized theologian, scholar, and the editor of The Companion Bible, we get:

> *Genesis 6:9 (TCB): "THESE are THE GENERATIONS OF NOAH: Noah was a just man and **without blemish** as to **breed and pedigree** in his contemporaries,"*

In Genesis 6:9, the Hebrew word for "perfect" is "tamiym" (תָּמִים), and means, "unblemished" or "without blemish". Interestingly, this word is used to describe the physical, without defect, genetically unblemished state of the animals used in the sacrifice of sin offerings (Exodus 12:5, Leviticus 1:10, 5:18, Numbers 29:2, etc.). Animals used in sin offerings were to be unblemished (genetically) or without defect. They had to be physically and genetically pure or "perfect" (Leviticus 22:20).

As bizarre as this may sound, Noah and his family were the last genetically pure humans on the planet. Otherwise, why would God's Word need to specify that the daughters, whom the angels of God mated with, were human?

> *Genesis 6:2 (NIV): the sons of God saw that the **daughters of humans** were beautiful, and they married any of them they chose.*

> *Genesis 6:4 (KJV): There were giants [Nephilim] in the earth in those days—and also after that—**when the sons of God came in unto the daughters of men**, and they bore children to them, the same became mighty men which were of old, men of renown.*

Most people assume that the sons of God were the descendants of Adam. But when we look closer we find that the sons of God were angels (Job 1:6, 38, 2 Peter 2:4-6) who came and took man's form so they could reproduce, perverting God's creation to spread a supernatural evil throughout the world.

This is not the only reference in God's Word of angels taking on man's form. We see examples in Genesis 19 and in Hebrews 13:

> *Genesis 19:1 (NIV): The two angels arrived at Sodom in the evening, and Lot was sitting in the gateway of the city. When he saw them, he got up to meet them and bowed down with his face to the ground.*

> *Hebrews 13:2 (NIV): Do not forget to show hospitality to strangers, for by so doing some people have shown hospitality to angels without knowing it.*

The sons of God could not be the sons of Adam because after Adam had fallen (who was a son of God or born in God's image), children were born in Adam's image or nature with a sinful flesh, not God's (Genesis 5:3).

Another common reason why theologians do not believe the term "sons of God" are referring to angels is because according to Matthew 22:30 and Mark 12:25, angels in heaven do not marry or reproduce. The problem with this theory, is that it doesn't take in account the domain that those angels are in: Heaven. We need to understand that there are two very different domains: Heaven and earth. Earth has sin; Heaven does not. These angels had fallen from their domain in Heaven (Jude 1:6) unto the earth where they were capable of perverting God's creation, including reproduction through marriage with humans.

When the angels fell from Heaven and mated with the daughters of man, they produced Nephilim. Nephilim is the Hebrew word "nĕphiyl" (נְפִיל), and means, "giant". Nephilim comes from the root word "naphal" (נָפַל), and means "to fall, lie, be cast down, fail, to fall violently, attack, to overthrow". Nephilim were the product of fallen angels from Heaven mating with the daughters of man. The super met the natural making the supernatural, producing an offspring of mighty giants (Genesis 6:4, Numbers 13:32-33).

> *Genesis 6:4 (NIV): when the sons of God came in unto the daughters of men, and they bore children to them, the same became mighty men which were of old, men of renown.*

We need to understand this was not a good "mighty". The "might" of the Nephilim was of an evil and violent nature. In other words, they were very, very evil and violent. Many theologians believe this is the origin of evil knowledge such as war, torture, and rape, for example.

The point of all this is to not get crazy into theology, but to understand that Noah lived during the most-evil of days this world has ever, and will ever, experience.

The reason these giants are not with us today is because God bound the angels so they could not pervert God's creation any longer.

> *Jude 1:6 (KJV): And angels who did not keep their own domain, but abandoned their proper abode, He has kept in eternal bonds under darkness for the judgment of the great day.*

The point of all this is to not get crazy into theology, but to understand that Noah lived during the most-evil of days this world has ever, and will ever, experience. It was not a natural evil, but supernatural. All because of God's gift of free will.

*Genesis 6:5-6 (KJV): Then the LORD saw that the wickedness of man was great on the earth, and that **every intent** of the thoughts of his heart was **only evil continually**. (6) The LORD was sorry that He had made man on the earth, and He was grieved in His heart.*

Every man on the earth was wicked. Not only were they wicked, but wickedness consumed *every* thought. When there is constant wickedness, there is no place for good. No humanitarian services, no charities, no churches, no good-deeds, just wickedness, everywhere, in every thought, all the time, except for Noah.

Can you imagine how wicked the world was that the God of perfect love and compassion was sorry that He had created humankind?

Genesis 6:6 (KJV): The LORD was sorry that He had made man on the earth, and He was grieved in His heart.

Can you imagine how wicked the world was that the God of perfect love was sorry that He had created humankind? Just think about it for a moment and let it sink in. Think about the magnitude of evil that would have had to be present for a loving, caring, giving, selfless, compassionate, perfect-creating God to get to the point where He grieved for what He had created. Something horrible must have gone wrong; something supernaturally horrible and evil. That is how evil the world was in Noah's day.

My point in telling the story of Noah and the Nephilim is to fully understand what was going on in the days of Noah and the flood. If anyone asks the question of how a loving God could kill His creation, we now have a small glimpse of what this world was like. And we will never know the supernatural evil of Noah's day. I believe modern day evil, such as Hitler and ISIS, aren't comparable to how evil this world was for a compassionate and loving God to condemn it.

People who question God's love in sending the flood are ignorant of not only just how wicked the world was, but the plan of Satan to keep us disconnected from God. God brought the flood out of mercy and love; that humankind would be reconciled to Him rather than being forever cut-off due to living in a world of pure wickedness.

People who question God's love in sending the flood are ignorant of not only just how wicked the world was, but the plan of Satan to keep us disconnected from God.

If this world would have continued to have been nothing but evil, there would have been no way for our LORD God and Savior to come because no woman would have been willing to carry the Messiah in her womb. The world tried to kill baby Jesus as it was. Imagine if every thought of every individual was wicked. God cannot force His Will on humankind (sovereignty) in that He has given us the gift of perfect love: Free will. God could not force our Savior into the world. Someone had to be willing to do good; to give life. And it was Mary.

How did the world become so wicked to the point that every man, but one, was evil? To answer this question, as well as in further understanding God sending the flood, it is vital to know what Satan had planned. This goes back to the curse of Satan in Genesis 3:

Genesis 3:15 (KJV): And I will put enmity between thee and the woman, and between thy seed and her seed: it shall bruise thy head, and thou shalt bruise his heel.

THINKING POINT

The plan of Satan was to forever cut humankind off from God. This is a similar reason why Adam and Eve were cast from the Garden of Eden. God placed cherubim and a flaming sword to guard the entrance so that man could not eat from the tree of life after they had been kicked out of the Garden of Eden as a result of eating from the tree of knowledge of good and evil. Immortality from the tree of life would have caused man to never die, living forever cut off from God.

Genesis 3 is prophesying that the "seed of woman" (Jesus) is going to "bruise" [crush] the head of the serpent (Satan), and the serpent is going to "bruise" [strike] the heel of the seed of the woman (Jesus). In other words, it is saying that Jesus is going to come and destroy the works of the devil (crushing Satan's head) through the crucifixion (Satan striking the heel of Jesus), as we just read in 1 John 3:8.

Satan knew one would be born to destroy him. He just did not know when He (Jesus) was coming, or even who He (Jesus) was going to be. As a result, Satan planned to keep the world cut off from God through keeping "woman" from bearing the Messiah, so that humankind would never be reconciled to God. Satan wanted to pervert the free will of man by introducing and spreading evil.

APPLICATION

Satan has no age limit on who he attacks in that he is interested in reproduction. For Satan, the earlier He can attack us, the better. He wants children born out of wedlock, he wants families destroyed by divorce, he wants children aborted. There is no child too young for Satan to attack. He even starts in the womb by bringing stress and fear on the mother.

But, thankfully, the power of God's love will always overcome evil. Gods plan for your life will always overcome any negative life experiences. Everything works out for the good of those who love God (Romans 8:28).

Satan knew he was finished when he heard the prophesy of Genesis 3. We can understand his motive in trying to kill the "seed of woman" before the seed had the opportunity to crush his head. This threat to Satan is why he had Cain kill Abel. Satan thought that Abel, who was living a righteous life pleasing to God through offering proper sacrifices, was "the seed of woman" who would crush his head. So, Satan got Cain, who was not living a life pleasing to God, to kill Abel before Abel had a chance to kill Satan, or so Satan thought. It is ironic that the first murder of humankind was over religion and is still happening today. Satan is still at work. Now, back to Noah.

> *Hebrews 11:7 (KJV): By faith Noah, being warned of God of things not seen as yet, moved with fear [respect], prepared an ark to the saving of his house;*

Noah heard from God when he was instructed to build the ark. Noah lived under God's instruction for 50 to 70 years, which is how long it took him to build the ark. That is a lifetime for us today. A lifetime of being obedient to God in preparing for something he had never seen before: Rain and floods (Hebrews 11:7). Not only did Noah have to prepare for something he did not understand, he had to do it in a world that hated what he stood for.

Because of his faith, Noah was a spectacle of God's work in an evil world. He did not have a safe-haven for a home, free from persecution as some of us have, or even a place to worship freely.

Noah was ridiculed, hated, and persecuted for what we know today as a lifetime, all for a purpose he did not know or understand. That, my friend, is faith. That is what you call putting beliefs into action; making decisions based on a confident expectation of God's goodness.

Noah didn't ask questions. He didn't make excuses and he didn't complain. Noah simply put his first foot forward in the direction where God was pointing him to go in a world that hated what he stood for and stayed the course for a lifetime.

> *Hebrews 2:4 (KJV): The righteous will live by faith.*

REAL LIFE

Justin and Renee's marriage is a story of faith. At first, Justin was scared to death to marry Renee. With a history of being unfaithful to every single woman, an addiction to alcohol and sexual promiscuity, he was hesitant to trust himself with a Proverbs 31 woman. Justin was even concerned about supporting her financially. He knew she was special and he truly didn't want to hurt her.

Renee on the other hand, had saved herself for marriage. In fact, after she recommitted her life to Christ, she did not date for 13 years! And now God brings her a man with such history? Not only that, but Justin was in college, living in his mother's basement, and had 3 daughters from a previous marriage. Not exactly prime bachelor material!

Needless to say, Justin prayed and fasted. God told Justin that He would not have given him Renee without giving him everything he needed, in Christ, to love and fulfill her. Renee also turned to God and she was able to see Justin as God did, as a new creation in Christ and not defined by his past.

INDIVIDUAL/GROUP DISCUSSION QUESTIONS

1. What is the difference between beliefs and faith? (Hebrews 11:1; p.80-81)
   _____
   _____
   _____
   _____

2. What is it that gives faith substance, or what is the process that gives faith tangibility? (James 2:14,17; p.81)
   _____
   _____
   _____
   _____

3. Why is the size of our faith irrelevant, and what does it mean when one has "great faith"? (p.88)
   _____
   _____
   _____
   _____

4. Why was Noah credited as having great faith? (Hebrews 11:7)
   _____
   _____
   _____
   _____

5. Why is it important to understand why the Bible would tell us that Noah was genetically perfect compared to the supernatural wickedness of the generation he lived in? (Genesis 6:5-6; p.91-92)
   _____
   _____
   _____
   _____

6. Why did a perfect, loving God kill off humankind with the flood? (Genesis 3:15; p.92)
   _____
   _____
   _____
   _____

7. Why was it Satan's goal to bring pure evil into the world to keep the "seed of woman" (Jesus) from being born? (p.93)
   _____
   _____
   _____
   _____

CHAPTER 7

IDENTITY: EXISTENCE + PURPOSE

7.1 YOUR NEW EXISTENCE

Identity is my favorite topic because there is no greater way to radically change or transform the life of an individual than by showing them who they are in Christ. The strength and authority of a Christian's life is established in their understanding of what Christ accomplished for them on the Cross, thus allowing them to *live in* God's intimate and perfect love for them. If there was one revelation I could give an individual and only one, it would be the magnitude of God's perfect love for them.

> When we take a belief system grounded in the truth of God's Word and we place it in action through our decision-making process (faith), we get substance to manifest as the very essence of our being in Christ: Our identity.

"Nothing binds me to my LORD like a strong belief in His changeless love." - Charles Spurgeon

When we take a belief system grounded in the truth of God's Word and put it into action through our decision-making process (hope-based faith), we get substance to manifest as the very essence of our being in Christ: Our identity.

Belief x Faith = Identity

If our beliefs are not rooted in God's Word, as well as lacking faith to put them into action, we will not have an identity rooted in Christ because there will be no substance to Christ being within us or our relationship with Him. However, the substance that gives life to our identity in Christ can be superficial. Even non-believers know how Christians should act.

When we hear about the substance of a Christian's identity, or in an identity in general, we hear common themes revealing identities being rooted in careers, being a father or mother, finances, accomplishments, playing a sport, a position held in ministry, serving in the church, and even mistakes made in life, for some examples. Although these are tangible expressions of who we are, specifically our behavior, we need to understand the difference in an identity being a natural fruit of who we are in Christ, rather than the superficial acts or behaviors used to obtain a perverted sense of self-worth, even when healthy.

A healthy manifestation of our identity in Christ will bring out the best in us because it will bring out Christ in us. A Christ-centered identity will show fruits that include holding a position in ministry, serving in the church, excelling at work, or being a father or mother, for example. But these same 'works' should never be the source of our identity or our self-worth. What we do should never be used as an attempt to gain right-standing with God. Self-righteousness is the purest form of unrighteousness, and it results from living under the law.

THINKING POINT

What do you place your identity in? Your profession? Your physical ability to play a sport? Your intelligence? Being a spouse? Perhaps it's what you own such as a nice car or boat? If any of these were taken away from you, what would happen?

I heard a saying that rang true along these same lines, and it is: "Those who put their identity in their looks will die a million deaths as they age." – Unknown. Regardless of what we place our identity in outside of Christ, some day it will come to an end and a significant part of us will die, creating an identity crisis. This identity crisis is why so many professional athletes, musicians, and movie stars experience depression after retirement.

There is one thing we can place our identity in that will last for an eternity, and that is who we are in Christ and His perfect love for us.

The problem is that in the flesh our identity is defined by our works (or mistakes), even our thoughts and emotions. In the spirit, our identity is defined by our Christ-like nature (John 14:20, 17:23, Ephesians 2:15, 1 John 4:17), created in God's image. What's difficult is getting the two to harmonize. The reason this is difficult is that our default mechanism to define ourselves is through our behavior, or flesh, because we tend to focus only on what we can see. This makes it easy to gravitate in measuring ourselves, even our relationship with God, by what manifests outwardly or through behavior, thus easily judging ourselves and others by what we do rather than by who we are in Christ.

There is truth to placing value on actions and behaviors, or on what we can see because faith without works is dead (James 2:17). However, behavior modification has been so taught and rehearsed in the church today that behaving as a Christian is common knowledge even to those who don't believe in Christ. It is easy to know what to do outwardly without engaging the heart and allowing God's love to be the motivator of our behaviors. Sadly, this lack of understanding keeps us from His personal process of development for our purpose of glorifying Him because behaviors that are rehearsed will never align with the nature in Christ.

We must understand that behaviors are not the problem; it's the 'how' or 'why' behaviors are originated. The origin of behaviors are influenced by beliefs, whether based on fear or the truth of God's love. Right(eous) believing will lead to right(eous) living, but this is very difficult to live out every day

> **Behaviors are not the problem; it's the 'how' or 'why' behaviors are originated.**

because it is our natural tendency to 'will' righteous behavior. It is natural for us to try and do righteousness ourselves apart from resting in the empowerment of the Holy Spirit.

REAL LIFE

Justin's education used to be a significant source of self-worth for him because he failed at everything else in life. The first thing he ever excelled at was being a student at the University of Minnesota. So, the day he graduated with two degrees and was no longer a student, he had a major depressive mood come over him. His identity as a student died, therefore his source of worth had died with it.

The way you overcome an identity established in anything other than Christ is through humility. It is only through Christ's healing and provision that Justin is the man he is today and can love his wife and children as Christ loves him. The more you realize how much God loves you, the more you realize that every good thing in life has come from God's Grace, because every good thing comes from Him (James 1:17).

We can often 'will' certain behavior for so long, aka willpower, but when we fail we expose ourselves to condemnation, guilt, and shame through being sin-focused because we failed to achieve "the mark" (Philippians 3:14). This guilt happens because when we try and earn righteousness through our willpower, we don't feel worthy of seeking God or entering His presence when we fail to act perfectly. This is the reason we need to believe who we are in Christ, so we can live out His nature.

Righteousness comes through belief and faith in Jesus Christ (Romans 3:22), and nothing else.

An identity crisis occurs when our behaviors do not align with what we believe. This is what is Biblically called being "double-minded" (James 1:8). The difference is rather than behavior being a source for our identity, behavior is a natural reaction (fruits of righteousness) to an identity established in God's love.

How does behavior become a result of our identity rather than it being our source? How do we get our behavior to align with what we believe? The answer is knowing and believing not only the Gospel of the Grace of God, but who we are in Christ (1 John 4:17). We find our true identity when we find ourselves in Christ.

The number one cause of an identity crisis is when we focus on sin. If focusing on sin produces an identity crisis because it contradicts our belief of being righteous in Christ, why do we focus on it? If the Gospel was about behavioral modification through willpower to correct sin, Jesus would have died in vain because the power to be sinless would be within us. We would have the ability to follow the Ten Commandments perfectly, but we cannot. When we ask God to work on our sin, we are asking Him to work on the part of us that God has already killed (through salvation) in the crucifixion of Christ (Galatians 2:20). Our identity is in Christ who has made *all* things new.

2 Corinthians 5:17 (KJV): Therefore if any man be in Christ, he is a new creature: old things are passed away; behold, all things have become new.

How have we been made new, without blemish? Notice how many passages are written about our being a new creation in Christ: Galatians 2:19-20, Colossians 2:12-13, Romans 6:2-7, 7:4-6, and Ephesians 4:21-24.

Now, when you add Romans 8:3-4, 12:2 and Philippians 3:10-11 to these verses, you can sum up what has taken place in 2 Corinthians 5:17:

> *2 Corinthians 5:17 (NIV): Therefore, if anyone is in Christ, he is a new creation; the old has gone, and all has been made new!*

In considering the number of verses there are on our being a new creation, do you think there is a proportional number of sermons on our new creation? Why not?

God does not resurrect our old, sinful flesh to clean it up. He works on our new identity in Christ; our new creation to teach us (conviction) how to live in His wholeness and finished works (Titus 2:12, Philippians 2:13, 2 Corinthians 12:9). The problem is that most of us don't really believe this because it really is too good to be true. That part of us that died with Christ was our sinful flesh:

> *Romans 8:3-4 (KJV): For what the law could not do, in that it was weak through the flesh, God sending his own Son in the likeness of sinful flesh, and for sin, condemned sin in the flesh: (4) in order that the righteous requirement of the law might be fully met in us, who don't live according to the flesh but according to the Spirit.*

Sins originate from our sinful flesh. Our sinful flesh has been condemned in the body of Christ and our sins have been forgiven (Psalm 32:2, Romans 4:8, 8:3).

> *Colossians 2:13 (NIV): When you were dead in your sins and in the uncircumcision of your flesh, God made you alive with Christ. He forgave us our sins.*

APPLICATION

We rarely self-reflect on the present. Our focus is either based on what we have done (past) or what we have going for us (future).

When you examine yourself in Christ, there will be two realities that you will gravitate to. You will either measure yourself by what you have done or who you're becoming.

When you focus on sin, you are focusing on what you have done. When you focus on who you are in Christ, you are focusing on who you are becoming in Christ and His purpose for your life!

Train your focus on who you are becoming in Christ, and don't let your past define you.

If our sins, past, present, and future have been forgiven and our sinful nature has been judged and executed in the body of Christ, what is left for God to see?

*Colossians 1:22 (NIV): But now he has reconciled you by Christ's physical body through death to present you **holy** in his sight, **without blemish** and **free from accusation**—*

We are not sinners saved by Grace. We *were* sinners, saved by Grace, made new, holy, and without blemish! You have been given new life upon salvation. This is your new existence!

*Romans 5:8 (NIV): But God demonstrates his own love for us in this: While we **were** still sinners, Christ died for us.*

Remember, sin does not make us a sinner any more than drinking water makes us a fish. This is the reason Paul says when he sins, it's not him:

Romans 7:17 (NIV): As it is, it is no longer I myself who do it, but it's sin living in me.

God sees us in Christ just as the Gospel of Grace says we are: Without blemish. If we see ourselves in any way other than what the Gospel of Grace says we are, we are believing a lie. Where is our identity rooted? In our old, dead, sinful self, or in our new creation created without blemish, in the likeness of God, made one with Christ (Ephesians 2:15)?

> God sees us in Christ as the Gospel of Grace says we are: Without blemish. If we see ourselves in any way other than what the Gospel of Grace says we are, we are believing a lie.

We are a new creation made in the likeness of God (Genesis 1:27, 1 John 4:17)! We try and raise ourselves from the dead every day when we ask God to work on the part of us that He already put to death in the body of Christ.

> Nowhere in the Bible does it say to work on our sin. In fact, the only 'work' we are told to do, is to labor to enter God's rest.

Christ died so the bad part of us would die with Him, that we would be resurrected with Christ Holy, perfect, and pure so we could have a perfect relationship with God. Why do we try and undo what God has so graciously done?

Nowhere in the Bible does it say to work on our sin. In fact, the only 'work' we are told to do is to labor to enter God's rest (Hebrews 4:11). In fact, the Bible says it is God who works in us to will and act out righteous behavior (Titus 2:12, Philippians 2:13, 2 Corinthians 12:9). Part of this 'work' we are called to do is putting off our old, dead self and putting on our new creation in Christ (Ephesians 4:22-24) through the renewing of our mind (Romans 12:2).

Behavior modification through willpower is not in God's Word. In fact, it says to work on our righteousness (new creation) through believing in Christ (Romans 3:22). The Bible does not deal with our dead man because it's dead. God knows it's dead because He watched it die in Christ. Dying with Christ and being resurrected with Him a new creation is God's Word. This is the Gospel of the Grace of Jesus Christ.

Grace is the presence of God that empowers us to become the very person He sees us as (Titus 2:12, Philippians 2:13, 2 Corinthians 12:9).

Christ dying on the Cross not only paid the price for our sins by taking our place at judgment, but He also became our sin, every sin, that we would be raised with Him perfect and without blemish. This great exchange is a demonstration of His love for us.

> **Grace is the presence of God that empowers us to become the very person He sees us as.**

To have an identity in God's love, we must know that His love has made us a new creation and that we are *worthy* of having a relationship with God because of Christs' perfect sacrifice on the Cross.

When we don't define ourselves by our behaviors and identify ourselves as a new creation in Christ, behaviors will align with our Christ-like nature, Christ's passions become ours and righteous fruits will naturally be produced (Galatians 5:22-23, 1 John 4:17). The result is an identity that is established in Christ, allowing us to live out our Christ-like nature. The more we realize God sacrificed Jesus to raise us up in Him, a new creation, righteous, all for His desire to have relation with us, the more we will know the magnitude of God's perfect love for us. And without this knowledge, we can't live as God created us to live in His perfect love (2 Peter 1:3).

7.2 KNOWING GOD'S LOVE

Knowing God's love for us is empowering because it fills us with the measure of the fullness of God in which there is a peace that passes understanding. And if you remember, peace is the precursor for everything God has for us.

> *Ephesians 3:19 (NIV): and to know **this love** that surpasses knowledge— that you may be filled to the measure of all the fullness of God.*

> *Philippians 4:7 (KJV): And **the peace** of God, which passeth all understanding, **shall keep your hearts and minds** through Christ Jesus.*

> **How do we teach or convey this peace and love that passes understanding? The answer is we exemplify it; we need to let it radiate from the very core of our being in Christ Jesus.**

How do we teach or convey this peace and love that passes understanding? The answer is we exemplify it; we need to let it radiate from the very core of our being in Christ Jesus. People will notice when God's love manifests through us into them. Love is very attractive. Even nonbelievers know when the hand of God is upon someone (Genesis 39:3).

We have got to know God's peace and love to be able to live it out. And this is a specific type of "knowing". "To know" God's love in Ephesians 3:19 is the Greek word "ginōskō" (γινώσκω), a Jewish idiom for sexual intercourse between a man and a woman.

> *Ephesians 3:19 (KJV): And **to know** the love of Christ, which passeth*

knowledge, that ye might be filled with all the fulness of God.

This knowing (ginōskō) passes mere knowledge. It's an experience, a state of being as one with another (Ephesians 5:31) just like in the marriage between a husband and wife. It's a specific connection that we have with an individual unlike any other in our life. It's the deepest, truest form of intimacy in a relationship, of knowing and interacting with another person.

THINKING POINT

When you are filled with the fullness of God, you are fulfilled, meaning there is no feeling of lack. You realize you have all you need in Christ (Psalm 23:1, James 1:4). If you think about this, we begin to understand that the times we make decisions based on fear are the times we feel we lack something or are fearful that we will go without.

When you are filled with the fullness of God you will not gratify the things of the world and your decisions and behaviors will reflect it!

REAL LIFE

A sweet example of God's perfect love is when Justin and Renee were selling a 3-meal backpack on Craig's List. It was a brand new $150 backpack that they hoped to sell for $100. It had a built-in cooler specifically designed for bodybuilders or people who enjoy fitness and desire to maintain their diet by prepping meals for each day. Justin bought this for Renee, but it turned out to be unsuitable for her at work. So, they decided to sell it.

After a month, they received a call from a lady who offered them $50. Justin and Renee were in a tight spot financially, yet wanted to sell it, so they countered at $75. The lady was very polite but declined as she was in a tough spot in her life. Immediately the Holy Spirit prompted Justin and Renee to give the backpack to her free. It was so evident that the Spirit may as well have spoken in an audible voice.

Justin and Renee didn't know anything about her, whether she was a believer or not, but Renee wrote a sweet note about God's love and placed it inside the backpack for her to find later. When the lady came to pick it up, she gave them a thank you card, letting them know that it was the day before her birthday and how this extension of kindness really touched her heart during this difficult time. That is God's perfect love.

When we truly comprehend the breadth of God's love for us at an intimate level, therein lies the fullness of God, our strength and empowerment because we will not gratify anything else except more of God's presence (Nehemiah 8:10).

God's love is a paradox in that it fulfills us to the fullest, but we can never get enough of it and will always want more.

> God's love is a paradox in that it fulfills us to the fullest, but we can never get enough of it and will always want more.

How do we get to know the love of God in such an intimate level as the analogy of being one flesh, or sexual intimacy, is used to describe it in Ephesians 3:19?

In General Systems Theory, the whole is greater than the sum of its parts and is shown as 1 + 1 = 3. This wholeness applies to our relationship with God as well.

1 (you) + 1 (God) = 3 (Wholeness/Fullness of God)

1 (you) + 1 (God) + _____ = 3 (Wholeness/Fullness of God)

What is the 3rd variable in the Wholeness Equation that equals 3? The answer is interaction! You cannot have intimacy with someone unless you have interaction.

You + God + ginōskō = Wholeness/Fullness of God (Ephesians 3:19).

To experience God's love as in being one with Him, we have got to interact with the Holy Spirit at an intimate level daily, much like a husband and wife. You have got to spend time in His presence, in His rest.

> Psalm 139:18 (NIV): How precious to me are your thoughts, O God! How vast is the sum of them! (18) Were I to count them, they would outnumber the grains of sand. When I awake, I am still with you.

God is so intimate with us that His thoughts for us outnumber the sands of the earth. He is so in-tune to our everyday life that He is there for us to direct our steps. Do

APPLICATION

The biggest problem that we can have in our relationship with God is complacency. We develop a passive relationship with God rather than an active one full of interaction. Do you go through everyday life just knowing God is with you in the back of your mind? Or are you filtering everything you see, hear, communicate, and act through the presence of the Holy Spirit?

What if a husband or wife tried to have an intimate relationship with their spouse, but knew nothing about them? It would be a relationship characterized by strife, frustration, disappointment, and conflict.

God knows us perfectly. He has done His part in being intimate with us. We need to do the same with Him through every thought of every day (interaction), otherwise we will be in a relationship with someone we don't know.

we spend as much time listening to Him as He does instructing us?

> *Proverbs 16:9 (NIV): In his heart a man plans his course, but the LORD determines (directs) His steps.*

7.3 YOUR EXISTENCE PURPOSED BY GOD

Before the beginning of time, God wanted a relationship with us. He created our existence, specifically, for us to know His goodness and to live in His perfect love. By taking the bad out of us, He made us a new creation in Christ for this to happen.

> *2 Timothy 1:9 (NLT): For God saved us and called us to live a holy life. He did this, not because we deserved it, but because that was his plan from **before the beginning of time**--to show us his grace through Christ Jesus.*

> *Ephesians 1:4 (NIV): For he chose us in him **before the creation of the world** to be holy and blameless in his sight. In love*

> *Titus 1:2 (NIV): in the hope of eternal life, which God, who does not lie, **promised before the beginning of time,***

Despite how your life came into existence, your existence has been purposed by God. We see this in Psalm 139:

> *Psalm 139:16 (KJV): Thine eyes did see my substance, yet being unperfect; and in thy book all my members were written, which in continuance were fashioned, when as yet there was none of them.*

Let us look at the Hebrew translation of Psalm 139:16:
  "My substance" is "golem" (גֹּלֶם): "embryo or fetus".
  "All my members" is "yatsur" (יְצֻרִים): "form, members [of the body]".
  "Which in continuance" is "yowm" (יוֹם): "lifetime".
  "Were fashioned" is "yatsar" (יָצַר): "formed or created".

Together we get: "Your eyes saw me as a fetus/embryo, being imperfect (born into sin), yet in your book you formed my body (your mind, soul, personality, character, etc.), and created my lifetime before it began."

God has literally written every day of your life in His book. He has literally seen it from beginning to end. Remember that God lives in a realm void of time (Psalm 90:4, 2 Peter 3:8). Also remember that He has seen every sin, past, present, and future, placing them in the body of Christ at the crucifixion (2 Corinthians 5:21).

Before you were formed, God not only knew you, but He also had a purpose for your life. That may seem incredible in itself, but it is even more mind-boggling when we consider genetics. If you remember in science class, the cellular division of meiosis produces gametes. Gametes have a single set of chromosomes or DNA and are in the form of a sperm (male) or as an egg (female). During fertilization, a mother's egg and a father's sperm (the gametes) fuse together to form a zygote, which then grows to become an embryo, and then a fetus or a child. In other words, one copy of the mother's DNA binds to one copy of the father's DNA resulting in an original, distinct, one of a kind human being.

The interesting part is the way the egg and sperm fuse together. According to how they fuse together determines the order of the genes of the child, therefore how the child will take form. This is because genes carry codes for what proteins are to be made and how much. It is the activities of these proteins within living cells and organisms that ultimately determines the individual's traits through gene expression (Brooker, 2005, p.385). Because the genes of the mother and father can assort and combine in numerous ways, there are over 8 million variations a child can express.

> *"Consider humans have 23 chromosomes per set. The possible number of different, random alignments equals 2^n (2 to the power of n), where n equals the number of chromosomes per set. Thus, in humans, this would equal 2^{23}, or over 8 million possibilities" (Brooker, 2005, p.57).*

Now, 8 million possibilities are specific to one couple. When you take into consideration the number of different mates a person can have, that number increases exponentially considering there are billions of people on earth. The possibilities of variations of children humankind can create are literally endless. This is the reason, scientifically speaking, there are no two people alike and why no two people have the same fingerprints. This is the creative detail of our God, and why we are loved specifically as we are. God created you before your existence came to be, and He created you for a specific purpose.

> *Ephesians 1:4-5 (NIV): For he chose us in him before the creation of the world to be holy and blameless in his sight. In love (5) he predestined us for adoption to sonship through Jesus Christ, in accordance with his pleasure and will—*

> *Ephesians 2:10 (NIV): For we are God's workmanship, created in Christ Jesus to do good works, which God prepared in advance as our way of life.*

In studying genetics, it is understood that both *genetics* and *environment* are essential for biological existence (Brooker, 2005, p.685). As children of God, our existence in this world is based on a similar principle in that our identity in Him (genetics) and His purpose for us (environment) comprises of our very existence or identity as being Christ-like. When looking at this, it makes sense when we understand what it means to 'exist'.

The definition of existence is, "reality as opposed to appearance", or "reality as presented in experience" (Merriam-Webster). To me, this reality means to function. The definition of function is, "the special purpose or activity for which a thing exists or is used" (Merriam-Webster). We have not only been purposed by God, but created for a specific function in this earthly realm.

> *Ephesians 1:11 (NIV): In him we were also chosen, having been predestined according to the plan of him who works out everything in conformity with the purpose of his will,*

> *1 Corinthians 12:27 (NIV): Now you are the body of Christ, and each one of you is a part of it.*

When you place existence in the context of function, you get a purpose or activity for your existence. Your identity, based on how God created you in His perfect love, is specific to fulfill His purpose for you which glorifies Him in that He is your Creator.

In other words, you were created for a purpose and your identity gives you the ability to function in a manner to fulfill that purpose, all in accordance to God's perfect will for your life (Ephesians 1:11). Through this mutual influence of purpose and existence, which an identity derives, you not only receive worth and meaning in knowing God was intimate in His creation of you, but you also receive worth and meaning knowing there is meaning to your existence. Our ultimate purpose is to glorify God (Isaiah 43:7) through functioning in the body of Christ (Romans 12:5-6, 1 Corinthians 12:8). Nothing will give you a greater sense of self-worth than knowing God created you with intention.

> *Isaiah 43:7 (KJV): Even every one that is called by my name: for I have created him for my glory, I have formed him; yea, I have made him.*

The place where we find this purpose of ours by God, is in His presence:

> *Psalm 16:11 (NIV): You make known to me the path of life; you will fill me with joy **in your presence**, with eternal pleasures at your right hand.*

REAL LIFE

Who is the One who knows you perfectly, including the desires of your heart? Who has a greater knowledge of the fullness of life than the God who created life? Many people can give the right answer to these two questions, but they will still turn to the foolishness of the world to attempt to satisfy their desires.

Justin lived in the bondage of being a slave to his desires. After all the different women he had been with, he thought he knew what he wanted in a wife. She never came. That lustful, fleshy desire and carnal knowledge kept him from ever being satisfied with one woman, no matter how beautiful or 'perfect' he thought she was. What he did discover, was that in the flesh or the world, perfection is an illusion and will never be attained by people, relationships, experiences, or material possessions.

Unexpectedly, Justin did experience perfection. He experienced the perfect love God has for him. Because God knows us perfectly, He can love us perfectly. And this is what most people fail to understand—that God knows us better than we know ourselves and knows what fulfills us even when we don't.

God put a woman in Justin's life that he didn't think he had any interest in whatsoever, and who had zero interest in him! Little did Justin and Renee know, God knew them so perfectly that He brought them together in marriage. When Justin and Renee thought they had an idea of who they wanted in marriage, God completely went the opposite way because He knew the desire of their heart better than they did. Renee is literally the only woman Justin has been faithful too, and he would have never chosen her. Renee would have never chosen Justin because she knew him in his past and despised him and how he lived. Renee even made comments to her friends that if God did 20 years-worth of work in his heart in a single night, she still would never consider me.

Justin and Renee's life is proof of the infinite love and wisdom of God; His perfect knowledge of who we all are and His desire to give us what we never knew we wanted: The desires of our heart. Renee was so in love with Jesus that she did not date for 13 years, because she was fulfilled being alone with God and because she trusted Him to bring the right man, at the right time, and in the right way. And God was faithful.

Being in His will is what living life to the fullest is because we are surrendering what we think is best for us and acknowledging God knows us better, and has a life waiting for us full of a fulfillment greater than what we ever thought we wanted or could achieve. God has a perfect purpose because we were perfectly created. All we must do is give control of our life to Him and He will amaze us beyond our wildest dreams.

7.4 AN IRRELEVANT PAST

When speaking of our purpose and existence, even our identity, it's important to understand that our past doesn't define who we are. When I say an "irrelevant" past, I am not saying there is not value in past experiences that God uses to grow and mature us, because there is. What I'm saying is no matter what we have done, what we have been through, or where we have come from, nothing can keep us from experiencing God's perfect love or fulfilling the purpose He has for us (Romans 8:38). Therefore, our past is irrelevant in that it does not define us or keep us from what God has purposed for our lives. The call and gifts of God are irrevocable (Romans 11:29).

When we don't have an identity rooted in the love of Christ, our default will be using behaviors and experiences of the past to define us. This default means of defining ourselves is why when we speak about purpose, we can automatically become critical of our past because we see it as limiting the potential of our future, or specifically, God's ability to use us. We must view our past as irrelevant while focusing on God's ability to bring us into what He has purposed for our future. Hurts are past tense. Hope is future tense.

> No matter what you have done, what you have been through, or where you are coming from, nothing can keep you from experiencing God's love or fulfilling the purpose He has for you.

Anytime the kingdom of darkness attacks us, the root of it will be aimed at our identity. Satan wants a believer in an identity crisis. The root of each lie he tries to get us to believe will be targeted at our identity and how we believe God sees us, because that will influence our relationship with God.

Satan's goal is to try and minimize who we are in Christ because God has empowered us through living in Him. Satan does not want us to realize that, in this world, we are like Christ (John 14:12, 1 John 4:17). He does not want us to know that we have the same power in us, through the Spirit, that raised Christ from the dead (John 14:12). Satan tried to kill Christ for a reason. Because Christ is in us, he is going to try to kill our Christ-like nature, and he attempts this through attacking our identity that is established in our belief of being one with Christ.

> Satan knows that if he can confuse our identity in Christ, he can confuse our life in Christ. The first thing Satan attacked in Adam and Eve, and in Jesus, was their identity.

Satan knows that if he can confuse our identity in Christ, he can confuse our life in Christ. The first thing Satan attacked in Adam and Eve, and in Jesus, was their identity.

> Genesis 3:5 (NIV): "For God knows that when you eat of it your eyes will be opened, and **you will be like God,** knowing good and evil."

> Matthew 4:3 (NIV): The tempter came to Him and said, "**If** you are the Son of God, tell these stones to become bread."

From the origination of life in the Garden, to Jesus hanging on the Cross, Satan had his eyes set on identity.

> Matthew 27:40 (KJV): "You who are going to destroy the temple and build it in three days, save yourself! Come down from the cross, **if** you are the Son of God!"

> When we focus on God and seek Him first, what we do or our behavior will naturally follow.

We cannot continue to look at what we do or what we have done to determine who we are. We confuse ourselves when we take our focus off God and focus on our past or our behaviors. When we focus on God and seek Him first, what we do or our behavior will naturally follow (Matthew 6:33).

Can you imagine if Paul let His past determine His identity? We probably wouldn't have most of the New Testament, if any.

> Philippians 3:13-14 (NIV): Brothers and sisters, I don't consider myself yet to have taken hold of it. But one thing I do: Forgetting what is behind and straining toward what is ahead, (14) I press on toward the goal to win the prize for which God has called me heavenward in Christ Jesus.

When Paul talks about a thorn in his flesh (2 Corinthians 12:7), some think it was a disease, others a Pharisee who followed him and challenged Him with theology. I believe the thorn in his flesh was the memories of his past, killing and tormenting those who are now his brothers and sisters in Christ.

Paul's context for Philippians 3, in forgetting what is behind him, is not to place confidence in the flesh. Confidence in the flesh not only consists of trying to obtain righteousness through 'works', but also in trying to understand the past to make sense of life, or to obtain meaning and value through understanding experiences.

> **In trying to make sense of the past, we are placing confidence in the flesh through understanding past behaviors to give substance to our identity and meaning to our life outside of Christ.**

In trying to make sense of the past, we are placing confidence in the flesh through trying to understand past behaviors or experiences in order to give substance to our identity and meaning to our life outside of Christ. This is of the flesh because our identity is based on our own knowledge and wisdom, rather than through belief and faith in Christ's love for us and being one with Him (Ephesians 2:15).

Hurts and pains live in the past. Anytime we try and understand behaviors of the past they will always seem illogical when seen through the lens of God's perfect, fulfilling love, or Grace.

THINKING POINT

After God revealed His perfect love to Paul on the road to Damascus, can you imagine what Paul must have gone through while reflecting on his past, reliving the memories of persecuting the very Gospel that has now given Him such joy and life?

Before Paul met God, Paul spent his life as Saul torturing, killing, and imprisoning those who are now his beloved brothers and sisters in Christ, people who he would now die for. Can you imagine how torturous that could have been for Paul if he 'lived' in his past or let it define who he was?

It is dangerous to try and understand the past let alone allow it to define who we are. We are not sinners saved by Grace. We *were* sinners saved by Grace (Romans 5:8), made new, perfect, and without blemish.

The enemy tries to steal our identity by getting us to place it in the things of this world rather than in God's love for us. An identity problem is a focus problem (Matthew 6:33).
We will either focus on who we think we are in the world or who God's Word says we are. Until we come into agreement with who we are in Christ, change will not happen.

Remember, salvation is learning to live out what we already are in Christ. Grace is the empowerment to live as God sees us. The Christian life is a journey of learning to live out our new creation in Christ through the empowerment of the Holy Spirit.

Salvation is learning to live out what we already are in Christ. Grace is the empowerment to live as God sees us.

This is the perfect love of God, that when we dwell in His love, righteousness will be the natural fruit of our life as we live out our Christ-like nature.

> *1 John 4:16-17 (KJV): And we have known and believed the love that God hath to us. God is love; and he that dwelleth in love dwelleth in God, and God in Him. (17) Herein is our love made perfect, that we may have boldness in the day of judgment: because as he is, so are we in this world.*

I want to make sure we understand that these negative emotions, feelings, and experiences that are associated with our past, affecting our identity, may not necessarily be acts that we have done, but have been done to us by the free will those we loved and trusted.

God does not orchestrate hurts and pains to teach us lessons. He doesn't have to. The only lesson He desires to teach us is to know who we are in Him.

APPLICATION

It can be difficult for us to understand that God knows us better than we know ourselves. God wrote our life in His book before our life even began (Psalm 139:16).

God has created you, specifically, for a purpose. He knows you perfectly; He knows what will fulfill you and what you will take pleasure in regarding your purpose. Will you trust Him? Many times when we are confused in life searching for meaning or not knowing what to do next, it is because we are focusing on the world. We are trying to understand what we think we would enjoy doing rather what we have been created to do in Christ.

Trust God, sit back and rest in Him knowing that He will open doors if you let Him. What God authors He finishes. He already has everything set up and ready to go for you. You just need to focus on Him and trust that He knows best.

It is important to understand that it's never God's desire for us to live a life of hurt and pain, or to be hurt, manipulated, cheated on, depressed, lied to, bailed on, or left behind. God does not orchestrate hurts and pains to teach us lessons. He doesn't have to. The only lesson God desires to teach us is who we are in Christ and how to live in His nature.

Let us review this Biblically:

Jeremiah 29:11 (NIV): For I know the plans I have for you," declares the LORD, "plans to prosper you and not to harm you, plans to give you hope and a future.

Harm is emotional, mental, or physical. God would never put us in a position to harm us mentally, physically, or emotionally. It's not His desire nor plan.

The Hebrew word for 'harm' is "ra`'" (רַע), and means "bad, malignant, unpleasant, displeasing, worse than, sad, unhappy, hurtful, wicked, misery, calamity, distress, adversity, injury, wrong, etc.". If you remember in our discussion on Job, "ra`'" (רַע) comes from the root word "ra`a`'" (רָעַע), and means, "evil".

Evil is the absence of a loving God. It's the absence of love; a void of love. There is no absence of God's love in His plan for us because it is not His nature. We know this because His plan for us is in His presence (Psalm 16:11).

If "evil" was a part of God's plan for our life or is His will for us to go through, how could we pray for the reconciliation or protection of marriages, for the kids of divorcing parents, for healing of sickness and illness, for the "evil" that strikes us? Would we not be praying in opposition to God's will? Do we think that God needs evil to be glorified; that His glory isn't magnificent or awe-inspiring enough without having pain and hurts to go through? To think that God causes hurts and pains are not logical; it just does not make sense.

> James 1:13 (NIV): When tempted, no one should say, "God is tempting me." For God cannot be tempted by **evil**, nor does he tempt anyone;

God is not the author of evil. He cannot tempt us with the absence of Himself, especially when the foundation of His Word is to seek Him first (Matthew 6:33) and that we are to be one with Him (Ephesians 2:15, 1 John 4:17).

God is the restorer. He is the rescuer, the shelter, and the rock. He builds up what has been broken down by evil and He does this in His presence.

We understand the origination of hurts and pains in our life when we look at what

Satan intends for us:

> God is not the author of evil. He cannot tempt us with the absence of His presence, especially when the foundation of His Word is to seek Him first (Matthew 6:33) and that we are to be one with Him (Ephesians 2:15, 1 John 4:17).

> John 10:10 (KJV): The thief cometh not, but for to steal, and to kill, and to destroy: I am come that they might have life, and that they might have it more abundantly.

To further understand God's loving nature and character, we need to eradicate beliefs that support this inaccurate theology of God orchestrating evil by examining the verses that are used to falsely support it. Our first example of a verse taken out of context is one we use to justify hurts and pains, or "evil":

> Isaiah 55:8-9 (NIV): For my thoughts are not your thoughts, neither are your ways my ways, (9) as the heavens are higher than the earth, so are my ways higher than your ways and my thoughts higher than your thoughts.

Most people use these verses to explain or justify their hurts and pains by attributing them to God, saying He is the one who willed or caused tragedy, sickness or illness to strike because "His thoughts and ways are higher than ours". Despite not understanding why bad things happen, they continue to credit God as the author of their hurts, pains, sickness, and disease. But this is not the context of the verse.

The context of Isaiah 55:8-9 is talking about God's radical Grace justifying the wicked (which we all were at one time I might add) because His ways are higher than ours. It is natural for us to take gratification when wicked people are punished, probably because in a fleshy or natural way it makes us 'feel' more righteous. To the contrary, God takes gratification when the wicked are reconciled to Him. This is difficult for us to understand because His thoughts and ways are higher than ours.

> *Isaiah 55:7 (KJV): Let the wicked forsake his way, and the unrighteous man his thoughts: and let him return unto the LORD, and He will have mercy upon him; and to our God, for He will **abundantly pardon** [justify the wicked]. (8) **for my thoughts** are not your thoughts, neither are your ways **my ways**, saith the LORD.*

THINKING POINT

What do you think the Bible means when it says to take joy in suffering (Romans 5:3 NIV)?

The word suffering in Romans 5:3 is the Greek word "thlipsis" (θλῖψις) and means "oppression". In the KJV, it is translated as "tribulations." In Hebrews 2:9, we see that Jesus was made a little lower than angels for the suffering of death. Why was Jesus put to death? Because he was rejected and persecuted. In fact, most of the time, if not every time, Paul uses the word "suffering" in the New Testament, it is in the context of persecution. Paul spent a lot of time in jail and, interestingly enough, this is when he wrote the most about being filled with joy. These writings are known as the prison epistles (Ephesians, Philippians, Colossians, and Philemon).

When God's Word tells us to take joy in suffering, it means for us to take joy in persecution just as Christ was persecuted unto death. It does not mean to take joy in poverty, sickness, illness, misfortune, calamity, etc. Remember, those are the definitions of "evil", or the absence of God and His perfect love for us.

As you grow in your boldness to proclaim the Gospel while getting a haircut, grocery shopping, or at your kid's ball game, you may encounter rejection or persecution. That is what we are to take joy in because we are being persecuted and rejected just as Christ was (Luke 17:25).

When it speaks of God's thoughts and ways being higher than ours, it's referring to God justifying the wicked. It's speaking of Grace and God's reconciliation of the wicked to a righteous standing through the blood of Christ. The context is not speaking of orchestrating hurts and pains in our lives to teach us lessons.

Are God's thoughts and ways higher than ours? Absolutely. But anytime we use these scriptures to attribute to God what is contrary to His nature and character, we are perverting His Word and condemning Him as the author of evil. Remember, this is what Job did; he blamed God for what was happening in his life (Job 40:8).

> Anytime we use these scriptures to attribute to God what is contrary to His nature and character, we are perverting His Word and condemning Him as the author of evil.

God is not the author of evil. He is the Author of love, fullness, and wholeness. The body of Christ was broken that we would be made emotionally, mentally, and physically whole. Remember God's response to Job's inaccurate beliefs:

> Job 40:8 (KJV): Wilt thou disannul my judgment? Wilt thou **condemn** me, that thou mayest be righteous?

It's much easier to blame God for negative experiences that we do not understand and bad decisions we have made, rather than opening our heart to the truth of God's nature and taking responsibility ourselves. This is called self-righteousness, the purest form of unrighteousness, because we base our righteousness on what we do rather than through belief and faith in Jesus Christ.

In a sense, we are saying we are more righteous than God because even though He is unjust according to His nature and Word in authoring evil, we will be more righteous by remaining devoted and obedient to Him despite what He is doing.

Let us address another verse of confusion:

> Philippians 4:13 (KJV): I can do all things through Christ which strengtheneth me.

Philippians 4:13 is not saying that we literally can do all things. If this were true, all of us Christians as a whole would not need to make up the body of Christ in which we have different roles and responsibilities (1 Corinthians 12:14). In a sense, one could argue that Jesus in the flesh could not do everything because He could only be in one place at one time (theoretically).

God sent the Holy Spirit upon us in Acts 1 so that we would go out into the entire world Christ-like, having the same power in us that raised Him from the dead (Matthew 28:19-20)!

Saying we can do all things in Christ who strengthens us gives people a false sense of hope that will have a bitter end

> Saying we can do all things in Christ who strengthens us gives people a false sense of hope that will have a bitter end when it seems as though God is not coming through or being faithful.

when it seems as though God is not coming through or being faithful. We each have different roles and responsibilities because we each have a specific purpose, and we see this in 1 Corinthians 12:20-22:

> *1 Corinthians 12:20-22 (NIV): But now there are many members, but one body. (21) And the eye cannot say to the hand, "I have no need of you", or again the head to the feet, "I have no need of you." (22) On the contrary, it's much truer that the members of the body which seem to be weaker are necessary;*

The context of Philippians 4:13 is saying we have the ability to persevere through all struggles and suffering because we are in Christ and He is our strength. This is seen in verse 11, where it says to be content in "whatsoever state" we are in. I believe God sends us more of His supernatural peace and joy when we are being persecuted, when we are content in Him during tribulations.

> *Philippians 4:11 (KJV): Not that I speak in respect of want: for I have learned, in whatsoever state I am, therewith to be content.*

The best way to see God's natural love and character is to understand what He had created before humankind had a chance to pervert it through free will.

Another way we can see why these verses are a source of inaccurate theology, that it is not God's desire or will to harm us, is to look at His original design. The best way to see God's natural love and character is to understand what He had created before humankind had a chance to pervert it through free will.

So, what was God's original design? It was the Garden of Eden. It was perfection; emotional, mental, and physical stability, security, provision, health, and wholeness. Most importantly, it was a place of perfect relation with God. Most people don't realize that what God had originally planned for us, before humankind had a chance to pervert it with free will, was perfect intimacy with Him.

However, God restored His original design. In the presence of the Holy Spirit that is within us, or intimacy with God, is where we still have this emotional, mental, and physical stability of God's peace, joy, and righteousness (Romans 14:17).

> *Romans 14:17 (NIV): For the kingdom of God is not a matter of eating and drinking, but of righteousness, peace and joy in the Holy Spirit,*

God is a God of perfection. He does not make mistakes, let alone author chaos, sickness, illness, death, sadness, misery, hurts, and pains. God is moved by the feelings of our infirmities, by our weaknesses (hurts and pains) because they are not His plan for us:

> *Hebrews 4:15 (KJV): For we have not a high priest (Jesus) which cannot be touched with the feeling of our infirmities; but was in all points tempted like as we are, yet without sin.*

When I feel distant from God, Hebrews 4:15 reminds me that God feels what I am going through and that is how intimate He is with me. He is there with me, experiencing what I am because He has gone through it as well as orchestrated a path out of it.

Why do we think God needs to bring us misery, calamity, and suffering to teach us His lessons or to reveal His goodness? Is His glory not enough? Is His presence not enough to radically change lives?

It's the goodness of God that draws man to Him (Romans 2:4). Don't ever stop being in awe of God's goodness and how much He loves you.

All the ick and filth we go through in this life is not authored by God, nor was it in His perfect, original design. It is authored by Satan (John 10:10), the deceiver and the father of lies.

Satan's goal is to keep us from interacting (intimacy) with God through living in fear and doubt of how much He really loves us.

> Proverbs 3:5-8 (NIV): Trust in the LORD with all your heart, and don't lean on your own understanding. (6) In all ways acknowledge Him, and He will make your paths straight. (7) Don't be wise in your own eyes; fear the LORD and turn away from evil. (8) It will be healing to your body and refreshment to your bones.

> Colossians 2:9-10 (KJV): For in him dwelleth all the fullness of the Godhead bodily. (10) And ye are complete in him, which is the head of all principality and power...

APPLICATION

I don't know about you, but it can feel as though God is distant when I am hurting, in emotional pain, sick, or simply not having a very good day.

What I fail to realize is that when I feel these negative emotions, despite what the source is, God is within me feeling what I feel. He is moved by my feelings of infirmities, my weakness, hurts, and pains.

God always identifies with what we are going through. In remembering this, it has helped me come to Him in those times when I simply don't feel like it. He desires us to come, He is our Comforter and wants to comfort us, but we need to come to Him to let Him because He will never force His will upon us.

INDIVIDUAL/GROUP DISCUSSION QUESTIONS

1. What is the cause of an identity crisis? (p.99)

_____

_____

_____

_____

2. When asking God to work on our sin, why are we asking God to work on our dead man? (Romans 3:22, Galatians 2:20, 2 Corinthians 5:17; p.100)

_____
_____
_____
_____

3. How do you convey a peace and love that passes understanding, or is beyond understanding? (Ephesians 3:19, Philippians 4:7; p.102)

_____
_____
_____
_____

4. Write the translation of Psalm 139:16 in your own words. (p.105)

_____
_____
_____
_____

5. How do we know that our existence has been purposed before creation? (Psalm 139:16, 2 Timothy 1:9, Ephesians 1:4, Titus 2:12)

_____
_____
_____
_____

6. Why is the target of Satan going to be our identity? (1 John 4:17; p.109).

_____
_____
_____
_____

7. How do we know that evil is not in God's plan; that it is the absence of God's presence? (Jeremiah 29:11, Matthew 6:33, 1 John 4:8; p.112)

_____
_____
_____
_____

8. When we attribute God as being the author of 'bad things' by saying "His ways are higher than ours", how do we know we perverting scripture (Isaiah 55:7-9) by using it out of context? (p.114)

_____
_____
_____
_____

CHAPTER 8

COMMUNICATION: HOLY SPIRIT INFLUENCE

8.1 PRAYING IN THE SPIRIT

The law is obsolete because we have been given a superior way of living righteously, and that is through living a Holy Spirit-influenced life (Romans 8:4). We exemplify the perfect love of Christ through living a Holy Spirit-influenced life. This is what we literally have been created to do. We are created to glorify God through living in His perfect love, allowing it to manifest through us into the world.

> We exemplify the perfect love of Christ through living a Holy Spirit-influenced life. This is what we literally have been created to do. We are created to glorify God through living in His perfect love, allowing it to manifest through us into the world.

The greatest and most powerful way for God's love to manifest through us into the world, is through praying in the Spirit. Communication with God fulfills the wholeness equation (1 you + 1 God = 3), in that communication is the third variable or the 'interaction' (ginōskō) component of the equation (1 you + 1 God + interaction = 3 Wholeness).

As we discussed, there are two doctrines that get attacked the most:

1. The Gospel of Grace.
2. Praying in the Spirit.

The enemy does not want the world to know the truth of these doctrines because of how radical, powerful, and life-changing they are. They are critical to living in the empowerment and influence of the Holy Spirit; to live Christ-like.

Most don't understand that to live a Holy Spirit-influenced life, we need to realize the *continual* need for us to be filled with the Spirit. For this to happen, we need to know the difference between our one-time-drinking of the water of life (salvation), and the need to be continually drinking, or in other words, to be continually refilled with the Holy Spirit.

In John 4, we see that salvation is a one-time-drink:

> *John 4:13-14 (NIV): "Everyone who drinks this water will be thirsty again, (14) but whoever drinks the water I give him will never thirst. Indeed, the water I give him will become in him a spring of water welling up to eternal life."*

Salvation produces a spring of living water that wells up from within us (from the

Holy Spirit), producing eternal life (quenching our thirst for eternity). This is a different, more personal "drinking" that is found in John 7:

> John 7:37-39 (NIV): Jesus stood and said in a loud voice, "Let anyone who is thirsty come to me and drink. (38) Whoever believes in me, as Scripture has said, rivers of living water will flow from within them." (39) By this he meant the Spirit, whom those who believed in him were later to receive. Up to that time the Spirit had not been given, since Jesus had not yet been glorified.

Here we see that Jesus is speaking of being thirsty. Initially, we might misunderstand the context of this verse as speaking of salvation in John 4:14. However, we know this is not true because those who drink the water of salvation will never thirst again. So, if one is saved, how can they be thirsty?

We see the context of John 7:37 in verse 39, that Jesus was speaking of being filled with the Spirit. Jesus was speaking of a different thirst than the thirst that is eternally quenched through salvation.

> Ephesians 5:18 (KJV): And be not drunk with wine, wherein is excess; but be filled with the Spirit.

When Ephesians 5:18 says "be filled with the Spirit", the "be filled" is the Greek word "plēroō" (πληρόω), and means, "to fill to the full; to supply liberally".

Why must something be supplied liberally? Because it is being exhausted, so to speak. To supply means to replenish. The phrase "be filled" is literally translated as "be being filled", meaning an active process or a continuation of an act. This shows us that being filled with the Spirit is a *continuous* need of ours.

APPLICATION

If you were to tell a Holy Spirit-filled Christian they needed to be refilled with the Spirit, you might have a very offended person. But the truth is, we all need to be filled with the Spirit on a continual basis.

It is not that the Spirit leaves us, but we become insensitive to the Spirit by simply living life in a wicked world. As long as we stay in God's presence, He will supply the Spirit to us liberally, more than we could ever need. But the times the world gets the best of you and you become stressed, angry, frustrated, upset, or sad, get back into the presence of God so that you can live above the circumstances through your empowerment in the Spirit!

So, how do we come to the place where we need to be refilled with the Spirit?

> Ephesians 4:30-31 (KJV): And grieve (affect with sorrow or suppress) not the Holy Spirit of God, whereby ye are sealed unto the day of redemption. (31) Let all bitterness, and wrath, and anger, and clamour, and evil speaking, be put way from you, with all malice.

When we dwell in anger or bitterness, for example, it makes us insensitive to the Spirit. We don't lose the Holy Spirit and He does not leave us, but we limit His ability to influence us as we focus on feelings and emotions that are not consistent with a belief in the loving nature and character of God. Becoming insensitive to the Spirit is called "grieving" the Holy Spirit, causing us to thirst again, thus resulting in the need to be refilled. So, how do we become refilled with the Holy Spirit?

> *Ephesians 5:18-20 (NIV): And be not drunk with wine, wherein is excess; but be filled with the Spirit. (19) Speaking to yourselves in Psalm and hymns and spiritual songs, singing and making melody in your heart to the LORD; (20) giving thanks always for all things unto God and the Father in the name of our LORD Jesus Christ.*

In Ephesians 5:19, we see that we are filled with the Spirit when we "speak to yourselves in Psalm and hymns and spiritual songs, singing and making melody in your heart to the LORD." To me, this is praying in the Spirit.

REAL LIFE

Two years after Justin came to know God, he and his wife went on a leadership retreat for the youth ministry they were serving. They were excited for God to use them because one of their passions is to influence and serve leaders. As is common with God, when ministering we end up receiving in return, and God ministered to Justin through a wonderful revelation.

During the retreat, worship was incredibly powerful because it was with those who genuinely loved to pursue God together. But God revealed to Justin a truth about who He is. Experiencing God while worshiping at the retreat was no different than the quality of worship he encountered when he was alone in his car, earnestly seeking Him.

This is not a testament to Justin, by any means, but of how God is faithful to reveal Himself when we seek Him *first*. His presence is the same no matter where we are or who were with. We don't need a worship band, to be at church or a retreat, we just need a heart that is purely seeking Him first in our life. He will show-up. He always does. He is faithful. He is within us.

Praying in the Spirit is a 'must' for a believer because it is through the Spirit that we are empowered, or that the power of God manifests through us into the world. Anytime the Bible speaks of power or being empowered, it is referring to being Spirit-filled. This is so important that Jesus instructed the disciples to wait for the promise of the Holy Spirit in Acts 1 before He commissioned them unto the world:

> *Acts 1:8 (NIV): but you will receive power when the Holy Spirit has come upon you; and you shall be My witnesses…*

Anytime the Bible speaks of power or being empowered, it is referring to being Spirit-filled.

THINKING POINT

One of the arguments I most commonly hear by those who don't believe praying in the Spirit is meant for believers today, is that this was meant for the early Church. They believe this gift ceased around the death and resurrection of Christ, or the gift of the Holy Spirit.

The reason I believe praying in the Spirit is a gift meant for us today, is because of the amazing results I have seen, along with my wife, during times in our life when we have been praying in the Spirit the most. The second reason is, the Bible says God does not change with the shifting of the shadows (Malachi 3:6, James 1:17). So, if God is the Word and the Word is God (John 1:1), and Jesus was the Word made flesh (John 1:14), then the Word hasn't changed and is still relevant for us today. This is the reason God's Word says it is eternal and will never change (Isaiah 40:8, Psalm 119:89, Matthew 24:35, 1 Peter 1:25).

Praying in the Spirit is for everyone. Paul thought so highly of praying in the Spirit that he let us know how much he did it and that he told leaders not to forbid it.

> *1 Corinthians 14:18 (NIV): I thank God that I speak in tongues more than all of you.*
>
> *1 Corinthians 14:39 (NIV): Therefore, my brothers and sisters, be eager to prophesy, and do not forbid speaking in tongues.*

Praying in the spirit is for everyone. Paul thought so highly of praying in the Spirit that he told leaders not to forbid it.

In the context of this study, we will be speaking of praying in the Spirit as an individual, private love language or prayer language, between ourselves and God, and is meant for everyday life. Now that we understand the need, let us understand why praying in the Spirit is so powerful.

Praying in the Spirit is powerful and effective because we are praying to God with the mind of Christ! Just think about that for a moment. We have the ability to pray with the mind of God!

Praying in the spirit is powerful and effective because we are praying to God with the mind of Christ!

> *1 Corinthians 2:10-11 (NIV): The Spirit searches all things, even the **deep things of God**. (11) For who among men knows the thoughts of a man except the man's spirit within Him? In the same way no one knows the thoughts of God except the Spirit of God.*
>
> *1 Corinthians 14:2 (NIV): For anyone who speaks in a tongue does not*

> *speak to people but to God. Indeed, no one understands them; they utter mysteries **by the Spirit.***

> *1 Corinthians 14:14 (NIV): For if I pray in a tongue, my spirit prays, but **my mind is unfruitful.***

Another reason praying in the Spirit is empowering is because we don't always know what to pray for, or even how to pray, especially in a future tense context. We see this in Romans 8:26:

> *Romans 8:26 (KJV): Likewise the Spirit also helpeth our infirmities: for we know not what we should pray for as we ought: but the Spirit itself maketh intercession for us with groanings which cannot be uttered.*

Praying in the Spirit allows us to pray God's purpose into existence. Being God is sovereign, it gives Him permission for His will to manifest into our life.

I don't know about you, but it can be difficult to anticipate what the LORD has for us, family, or friends. Praying in the Spirit allows us to pray God's purpose into existence.

Being God is sovereign and cannot force His will upon us, praying in the Spirit gives Him permission for His will to manifest into our life, for doors to be opened and opportunities to arise, for new seasons to begin. It allows God to bring dead areas in our life to life. This is the reason the Bible says He will answer our prayers when we pray in accordance to His Will (1 John 5:14-15).

Think how important this is when we don't know what to pray for. This weapon is so powerful that we can pray to God with His own mind, agreeing with His desire to break bondages in life, to bring healing, restoration, peace, joy, and righteousness.

In Romans 8:26, we also see the intimate context of praying in the Spirit when it says the Spirit makes intercession for us with "groanings" which cannot be uttered. This "groaning" means a soft utterance; a soft sigh or a whisper as if whispering to God in a private love language.

The "deep things of God" is a metaphor for the deep, personal, intimate thoughts of God; His perfect will or passion for us that resonates from His heart.

> *1 Corinthians 2:12-13 (NIV): We have not received the spirit of the world but the Spirit who is from God, that we may understand what God has freely given us. (13) This is what we speak, not in words taught us by human wisdom but in words taught by the Spirit, expressing spiritual truths in spiritual words.*

When we are praying in the Spirit and the Spirit intercedes for us uttering the mysteries of God's heart, we are expressing spiritual truths in spiritual words. Your life is a spiritual truth because it has been written in God's book before you even came to be (Psalm 139:16). You are praying for his plan to manifest in your life. We have got to pray in the Spirit to access the mind of Christ for our heart to make melody with His and for his path for our life to be revealed (Psalm 16:11)!

THINKING POINT

Scientific research shows that when we pray in the Spirit we, in fact, are not praying with our mind (1 Corinthians 14:14).

This was found by a self-proclaimed agnostic researcher, Andrew Newberg, MD, of Pennsylvania School of Medicine (Newberg, 2006). Newberg states, "We noticed a number of changes that occurred functionally in the brain. Our finding of decreased activity in the frontal lobes during the practice of [praying in the spirit] is fascinating because these subjects truly believe that the Spirit of God is moving through them and controlling them to speak. Our brain imaging research shows us that these subjects are not in control of the usual language centers during this activity, which is consistent with their description of a lack of intentional control while [praying in the spirit]. These findings could be interpreted as the subject's sense of self being taken over by something else. We, scientifically, assume it's being taken over by another part of the brain, but we couldn't see, in this imaging study, where this took place" (Newberg, 2006).

When we pray in the Spirit:

1. We are praying to God (1 Corinthians 14:2).
2. We are praying with the mind of Christ (1 Corinthians 14:14).
3. The Spirit makes intercession for us (Romans 8:26).
4. We give God permission for His Will to manifest in our life.

When we are praying in the Spirit, we are praying for God's will to manifest in our life, for His passions to become ours, for bondages to be broken, and for direction to be given. This may be hard to believe, but God does not intend for us to go through this life in the dark or wearing a blindfold, guessing what is next. Intimacy creates familiarity, and this includes the thoughts and desires of God for our life.

> Intimacy creates familiarity, and this includes the thoughts and desires of God for our life.

Along with reading God's Word, praying in the Spirit taps us into the knowledge of God. Some of the greatest questions I asked God were answered through fasting or in simply worshiping Him. We tap into His knowledge and understanding through being in His presence.

> Some of the greatest questions I asked God were answered through fasting or simply in worshipping Him.

1 Corinthians 2:15-16 (NIV): The person with the Spirit makes judgments about all things, but such a person is not subject to merely human judgments, (16) for, "Who has known the mind of the LORD so as to instruct him?" But we have the mind of Christ.

God values knowledge and has given it to us for everyday life (2 Peter 1:3). God acknowledges how critical it is for us to have His knowledge because living without it results in destruction.

> Hosea 4:6 (KJV): My people are destroyed for lack of **knowledge**: because thou hast rejected knowledge,
>
> 2 Corinthians 8:7 (KJV): Therefore, as ye abound in everything, in faith, and utterance, and **knowledge**, and in all diligence, and in your love to us, see that ye abound in this grace also.
> Philemon 1:9 (KJV): And this I pray, that your love may abound yet more and more in **knowledge** and in all judgment;
>
> Colossians 1:9 (KJV): and to desire that ye might be filled with the **knowledge** of his will in all wisdom and spiritual understanding;

REAL LIFE

When speaking of knowledge, it is important to understand Israel's, God's chosen people, wealth of knowledge poured out upon them in abundance by God. In the over 100-year history of the Nobel Prize, Israel has won in an abundance and is reflected in percentages completely out of proportion to their population size compared to other nations. Jews constitute approximately 20% of all Laureates despite being 0.19% of the world's population, with almost three times the number of awards won by either Germany or France (including their Jewish winners), and 10 times those won by Japan (Kopf (2002).

> Colossians 1:10 (KJV): That ye might walk worthy of the LORD unto all pleasing, being fruitful in every good work, and increasing in the **knowledge** of God;
>
> 2 Peter 1:3 (KJV): According as his divine power hath given unto us all things that pertain unto life and godliness, through the **knowledge** of him that hath called us to glory and virtue:

Believers have way too many questions concerning their life. God desires us to have His knowledge. Does this mean we are all going to become geniuses? Most likely not. Does this mean we'll know where we'll be in five years? Probably not.

God will give us knowledge pertaining to what He has purposed for our life. This may be a blessed mind to succeed at a job, an innovative idea concerning a profession, or it may mean understanding some of our life experiences, thus deriving wisdom from them so we don't repeat mistakes. What I can guarantee is that it pertains to His Grace and in understanding His perfect love for us, His love for the world, and how He sees us in Christ.

My point is, life makes sense in God's presence where there is understanding. God is not a god of chaos, confusion, or secrets. He is a God of all knowledge, understanding, and wisdom. And we have access to His mind when we pray in the Spirit and worship Him. This knowledge that pertains to what God has purposed for us is what 1 Corinthians 2:13 is speaking of:

> *1 Corinthians 2:13 (NIV): This is what we speak, not in words taught us by human wisdom but in words taught by the Spirit, expressing spiritual truths in spiritual words.*

The phrase "expressing spiritual truths in spiritual words" is Greek for "pneumatikos" (πνευματικός), and means, "relating to the human spirit, or rational soul, as part of the man which is akin (related) to God and serves as His instrument or organ". As we recently discussed, our life is a spiritual truth because God wrote it into existence before we were even created (Psalm 139:16).

> *Psalm 139:16 (NIV): Your eyes saw my unformed body; all the days ordained for me were written in your book before one of them came to be.*

Our life, a spiritual truth, is an instrument or organ of God in the body of Christ that has been created to fulfill the perfect will of God through what He not only has purposed for our life, but also through living as Christ did in this world (1 John 4:17).

> **Our life, a spiritual truth, is an instrument or organ of God in the body of Christ that has been created to fulfill the perfect will of God through what He not only has purposed for our life, but also through living as Christ did in this world.**

The reason praying in the Spirit is powerful is that when we pray in the Spirit, we are praying His will for our life to manifest in the present, here and now. We are praying that God's spiritual truth for our life, our purpose as His instrument or organ, would come to manifest today! This is huge! This is where breakthroughs happen, because it is important when it comes to God answering prayers. Why?

> **God does not say He will give us anything we ask for because in order for Him to hear us, we need to be asking in accordance with His Will.**

*1 John 5:14 (NIV): This is the confidence we have in approaching God: that if we ask anything **according with his will**, he hears us.*

One of the reasons prayers are not answered is because we are praying for things that are not in God's Will for us. God does not say He will give us anything we ask for because for Him to hear us, we need to be asking in accordance with His Will (1 John 5:14). God will never answer a prayer of ours that is not in accordance to His Will.

When we pray in the Spirit, we are praying for God's perfect Will to manifest in our life. Praying in the Spirit is so powerful because we are praying in accordance with His Will. And when we pray in accordance to His perfect Will, He will move!

Some of the greatest times God has moved in my life has been directly related to the times that I have been praying in the Spirit the most. We need to pray in the Spirit to make sure we are praying in accordance with God's perfect Will because we do not always know what to pray for.

> *Romans 8:26 (KJV): Likewise the Spirit also helpeth our infirmities: for we know not what we should pray for as we ought: but the Spirit itself maketh intercession for us with groanings which cannot be uttered.*

We are unaware of the things that God has prepared for our lives. We are also unaware of what Satan has planned for us. It is good that we don't know either of these plans. We are already impatient as it is, just imagine how we would be put into a craze if we knew what the future held for us? Would we have the patience to let God mature, develop, prepare, and teach us for what He has purposed? I know I wouldn't! I would want it now.

On the other hand, what if we knew what Satan had planned for us? If I knew what Satan had planned for my wife or my children, I probably would keep them locked up at home because I would want to protect them and keep them safe.

An example of not knowing what to pray could be praying for something to come into our life that would cause us harm. An example of this is money. A majority of lottery winners end up bankrupt within years after winning. What they 'willed' into their life caused them to become worse off than before their 'will' came true. God will not answer a prayer that He knows will cause us harm or that we are lacking the maturity to handle.

Even when we know what to pray for, it can still be difficult. Praying in the Spirit enables us to pray in full assurance of faith in times when it can be difficult to pray in faith. When our mind is disengaged, it cannot contend against what we're praying for due to stress, fear, or unbelief.

> **Effective prayer happens when we align our heart with the Holy Spirit. When our heart aligns with the direction and purpose God has for our life, we are in His Will. A pure heart is when our desires align with the desires of God, and His passions become ours.**

Effective prayer happens when we align our heart with the Holy Spirit. When we align our heart with the direction and purpose God has for our life, we are in His Will (1 John 5:14). A pure heart is when our desires align with the desires of God and His passions become ours (Psalm 24:3-5, 51:10, Matthew 5:8).

Not only does praying in the Spirit bring God's Will into reality through aligning our heart to His, but it also heals us (Jude 1:20, Romans 8:26).

> *1 Corinthians 14:4 (KJV): He that speaketh in an unknown tongue edifieth himself; but he that prophesieth edifieth the church.*

APPLICATION

I have heard individuals denounce praying in the Spirit because they took 1 Corinthians out of context, thinking it tells us not to pray in the Spirit because it 'exalts' us. They believe that it is a sin for us to be exalted.

But did you know that it is God's desire to exalt us? We see this in Joshua 3:7, Psalm 75:10, and especially in James:

James 4:10 (KJV): Humble yourselves in the sight of the LORD, and he shall lift you up.

The more He lifts you up, the more humbling it is because you know it is not because of you but because of His goodness and love for you.

For some reason when people read this verse, they think the word 'edifieth' means exalted. They assume this verse is saying it is not good to exalt oneself because we should be exalting the church or God instead. This is not what this verse is saying. The Greek word for "edifieth" is "oikodomeō" (οἰκοδομέω), and means, "to build a house, restore, to build, to repair".

When we pray in the Spirit we are restoring our temple, which is our body and mind (1 Corinthians 6:16). We are healing our body and mind at the cellular level. And since we are a part of the body of Christ, God desires to edify us to edify His church. What keeps our healing from fully manifesting is when we return to the thoughts and behaviors that He is healing us from.

THINKING POINT

The edification of our body and mind that happens through praying in the Spirit is also reinforced by scientific research:

Carl R. Peterson, MD, a brain specialist and psychiatrist, conducted a study on praying in the Spirit at Oral Roberts University, in Tulsa, Oklahoma. What he found was astonishing. Through his research, we now know that praying or worshiping in the Spirit activates parts of the brain that has no other apparent activity known to science. This specific, unique area of the brain that is only activated by praying in the Spirit, releases two chemical secretions that flood the immune system and boost its productivity 35-40%, thereby promoting the healing that takes place in our bodies (Peterson, 2011), physical and mental. Later in the article, Peterson associates the benefits of praying in the Spirit as similar to the effects of exercising, such as reducing stress levels in the body, the brain releasing health-benefiting endorphins, and significantly reducing blood pressure.

A very significant percentage of the central nervous system is directly and indirectly activated in the process of extended verbal and musical prayer over a period of time. This results in a significant release of brain hormones which, in turn, increase the body's general immunity. It is further enhanced through joyful laughter with increased respirations and oxygen intake to the brain, diaphragm, and other muscles. This same phenomenon is seen in physical activity in general, i.e., running, etc. (Peterson, 2011).

Another example is a study that collected saliva samples to measure stress hormones from sixty participants that prayed in the Spirit. "The data suggest that glossolalia (praying in the Spirit) is suggestively associated with a reduction in stress in response to normal stressors, and significantly associated with positive mood and calmness. This supports the growing body of work validating the health-improving effects of religiosity and the claims of Pentecostals themselves" (Lynn, 2009).

Praying in the Spirit:

1.   Fills us or sensitizes us with the Spirit.
2.   Prays the perfect Will of God to manifest in our everyday life.
3.   Edifies or heals our body, therefore builds up the Church.

There is a fourth benefit to praying in the Spirit, and it involves our protection.

8.2 THE DOUBLE-EDGED SWORD

The fourth benefit to praying in the Spirit has to do with not only our protection, but is also the only offensive weapon we have in the armor of God:

> *John 7:37-39 (KJV): In the last day, that great day of the feast, Jesus stood and cried, saying, if any man thirst, let him come unto me, and drink. (38) He that believeth on me, as the scripture hath said, out of his belly shall flow rivers of living water. (39) (But this spoke He of the Spirit, which they that believe on Him should receive: for the Holy Ghost was not yet given; because that Jesus was not yet glorified).*

When we pray in the Spirit, what do we have flowing from our belly or innermost man? The answer is rivers of life! When we pray in the Spirit, we have rivers of living water flowing out of us from our belly or our "innermost being". These rivers of living water are very interesting when we take into consideration Ephesians 6:16:

> *Ephesians 6:16 (KJV): Above all, taking the shield of faith, wherewith ye shall be able to **quench** all the fiery darts of the wicked.*

What quenches fire? Water, or the rivers of life! Praying in the Spirit generates rivers of living waters that are a shield of faith protecting us from the enemy.

When speaking of the armor of God, we see that praying in the Spirit protects us or is a defense from the attacks of the kingdom of darkness. However, praying in the Spirit and speaking God's Word into our life are also the only offensive weapons in the armor of God.

> *Ephesians 6:17 (KJV): And take the helmet of salvation, and the sword of the Spirit, which is the Word of God:*

Throughout this study, we have discussed that the Word of God and the Holy Spirit are synonymous (Hebrews 4:12).

> *Hebrews 4:12 (KJV): For the Word of God is quick, and powerful, and sharper than any two-edged sword, piercing even to the dividing asunder of soul and spirit, and of the joints and marrow, and is a discerner of the thoughts and intents of the heart.*

Look closely in Hebrews 4:12 (KJV) to where it says "sharper than any two-edged sword". The word "two-edged" in Greek is "distomos" (δίστομος), and means, "a river having a double mouth". I know, weird, right? But that's its Greek meaning.

When we are praying in the Spirit, we are using our mouth and the mouth of the Spirit, thus creating the double-mouthed river, or the two-edged sword. One edge is our mouth speaking truth, the second edge is the mouth of the Holy Spirit speaking through us or interceding as we previously learned.

Now, the two-edged sword has a double purpose in our life. Not only is praying in the Spirit a two-edged sword, but so is speaking God's Word over our life. The offensive weapon of the two-edged sword happens when:

1. We pray in the Spirit.
2. We speak the Word of God over our life and the life of others.

In both these situations we are taking hold of the two-edged sword. One edge of the sword is God's Word, being He spoke it, and the second edge is when we speak it over ourselves or over our family and friends. To speak God's Word with authority, it is crucial to know God's Word, receiving it in our hearts, enabling us to use it as a weapon in our lives by speaking it into our life and the lives of others.

Speaking God's Word into reality, along with praying in the Spirit, is a critical, powerful weapon God has given us to live empowered in His perfect love.

Speaking God's Word into reality, along with praying in the Spirit, is a critical, powerful weapon God has given us to live empowered in His perfect love. When we use our two-edged sword through either speaking God's Word or praying in the Spirit, we sever the bondages of the kingdom of darkness in our life. We sear the chains of addiction, abuse, anger, hurt, poverty, stress, sickness, and disease.

APPLICATION

It is easy for us to think that God is measuring us to see if we sin or not. Why do we believe this if, in God's eyes, our sins do not exist because they have been forgiven, and our sinful flesh condemned in the body of Christ? The reason why God measures us is not to see if we sin, but to give us increase!

God measures us to see if we are receptive to Grace (10 Lepers in Luke 17) and how sensitive we are to Holy Spirit direction or influence (Ezekiel 47). When God measured Ezekiel in the river of life, He began with the river at his ankles, and then it moved to his waist, finally engulfing his entire body. Ezekiel in the river of life is symbolic of us being in the Spirit, and we know this because water is a symbol of the Spirit. If God measures us by these means, perhaps we should, too!

God wants us so engulfed in the Spirit as if we were engulfed by a fast-moving river being led by its current. When we let the current take us, it will take us to the east (Ezekiel 47:1) which is the manifestation of God's glory (Ezekiel 43:2)!

Self-reflect daily to see how receptive you are to Grace and Holy Spirit direction. Empowerment happens when we take our focus off of sin and place it on Jesus Christ (Matthew 6:33), aligning our heart desires with His through Holy Spirit influence.

Praying in the Spirit and reading God's Word have similar, powerful effects of directing our lives and enabling us to make decisions with the knowledge and wisdom of God in our decision-making process. When we read God's Word, taking it to heart, we are in His presence and we have a lamp upon our life.

>*Psalm 16:11 (NIV): You make known to me the path of life; you will fill me with joy in your presence, with eternal pleasures at your right hand.*

>*Psalm 119:105 (NIV): Your word is a lamp for my feet, a light on my path.*

8.3 THE WEAPON OF THANKSGIVING

Praying in the Spirit, or speaking to ourselves in Psalm, hymns, and spiritual songs, is not the only way to be filled with the Spirit. The second way that many may not realize, is quite simply to give thanks.

>*Ephesians 5:18-20 (NIV): And be not drunk with wine, wherein is excess; but be filled with the Spirit. (19) Speaking to yourselves in Psalm and hymns and spiritual songs, singing and making melody in your heart to the LORD; (20) **giving thanks** always for all things unto God and the Father in the name of our LORD Jesus Christ.*

The greatest, most powerful way for us to communicate with God is to thank Him for everything in our life. Giving thanks is the Will of God (1 Thessalonians 5:18). Giving thanks helps us focus on God's goodness and what He has done in our life during the times when it's easy to lose sight on His goodness. Giving thanks helps us focus on His love and Grace. It acknowledges His goodness in our life (1 Thessalonians 5:18, Ephesians 5:20, James 1:17).

> Giving thanks helps us focus on God's goodness and what he has done in our life during the times when it's easy to lose sight of His goodness.

To understand the power of thanksgiving, we will look at two stories in the Bible:

1. When Christ fed the 5,000.
2. When Christ cleansed the ten with leprosy.

The feeding of the 5,000 is the only miracle that is recorded in all four gospels (Matthew 14, Mark 6, Luke 9, and John 6). This tells us there is something special about this miracle; the power of thanksgiving.

The Book of John (Chapter 6) says that Jesus gave thanks then distributed the fish and bread. Matthew 14, Mark 6, and Luke 9 show us that Jesus blessed the fish and bread then distributed them. Why the difference? Why the discrepancy in God's Word between giving thanks and blessing the bread and fish?

When we give thanks, we are blessing what we are thankful for. Not always quantitatively such as in finances, but it can also be qualitatively such as God increasing enjoyment in relationships or marriages.

Thanksgiving is also evident in the story when Jesus healed the ten with leprosy in Luke 17, as we previously discussed briefly. In reading the story, we see that the ten lepers were cleansed and healed from leprosy as they were going to show themselves to the priest, as directed by Jesus.

> **When we give thanks, we are blessing what we are thankful for.**

In Luke 17:15 we see that when one realized he was healed, he turned back to Jesus and glorified God. In other words, he gave thanks. God wants us to be thankful. Why?

Thankfulness is humility. People who are not humble are not able to be thankful for what they have been given.

> **People who are prideful are not able to receive the Grace God has freely given them because they believe they have earned it.**

People who are prideful are not able to receive the Grace God has freely given them because they believe they need to earn it or have earned it. An ungrateful heart believes it deserves what it has been given. The root is believing we have achieved what we have been given based on our ability. An ungrateful heart fails to acknowledge God's Grace, the very power of salvation, which is His unmerited favor and love for us. This goes back to the obligation principle in Romans 4:

> *Romans 4:4-5 (NIV): Now to the one who works, wages are not credited as a gift but as an obligation. (5) However, to the one who does not work but trusts God who justifies the ungodly, their faith is credited as righteousness.*

APPLICATION

One of the ways the enemy brings temptation upon us is to get us to focus on what we don't have. Giving thanks changes our focus from what we don't have to everything that God has given us. The reason this is so powerful is that it acknowledges God's goodness in our life. It is a means to make faith effectual because we begin to see the fruits of our hope, God's goodness in the things that we enjoy in life.

Besides, do you think Adam and Even would have sinned if they would have focused on everything God had freely given them (Grace) through giving thanks, rather than focusing on the one thing they didn't have, the fruit of the tree of knowledge of good and evil?

When the one leper returned and gave thanks for His healing, something incredible happened: He was made whole. The leper was healed when he believed in Christ for healing; he was made whole when he gave thanks for what God had done.

> *Luke 17:19 (KJV): And He said unto him, Arise, go thy way: thy faith hath made thee whole.*

The reason giving thanks to God for the things in our life is so powerful is because we are making our faith effectual.

> Philemon 1:6 (KJV): That the communication of thy faith may become effectual by the acknowledging of every good thing which is in you in Christ Jesus.

When we give thanks to God, we are putting our beliefs into action. We are making our faith "effectual" by acknowledging God's goodness in our life.

When we give thanks to God, we are putting our beliefs into action. We are making our faith "effectual" by acknowledging God's goodness in our life (James 1:17). Giving thanks glorifies God in that it acknowledges, through our belief, the manifestation of His presence in our life.

THINKING POINT

Along with the words we use, communication is very powerful. This is because we define our life through the words we chose to use, or in 'language', that gives sense and meaning to life, or lack thereof. There is a reason for this, and an important one. Problems, though manifested in the mind or the physical, exist in language [which is used to construct and describe experiences, such as problems], through a web of meaning created by those who engage in dialogue about the problem (Griffith et al., 1990). The reason this co-creation of reality (this dialogue we have with others, even ourselves) is important, is because problems are reinforced and strengthened when beliefs are formed or grow alongside the problems. Using language that has been developed around experiencing a problem will reinforce problematic behavior, leading to more thoughts and behaviors that will continue to support the problem.

In other words, the language you chose to use to describe experiences or problems will reinforce beliefs that can compound, worsen, justify, and strengthen the manifestation of problematic behaviors, or barriers to experiencing God's perfect love. How you perceive your behavior through your language will also reinforce or increase its manifestation. The language you choose to use can serve as a barrier to living in God's perfect love. To the contrary, using the language of God's Word can be used to conquer these strongholds. This is one of the reason why God's Word says the tongue has the power of life or death (Proverbs 18:21). The language you choose to use will bring life or death upon you.

Changing the 'language' you choose to use about your life, in accordance to God's Word, will co-create a new reality that will sever the bondages in your life, enabling you to live in God's perfect love. There is no better language to use to speak into your life, to describe your life, than the language of God's Word.

REAL LIFE

Justin and Renee's testimony paints a beautiful picture of the hand of God literally bringing them together in marriage. This was not only seen on the canvas of their lives, but also through their diligent prayers and pursuit of the Holy Spirits direction. Renee is a prayer warrior and spent countless hours praying, seeking counsel and prayers from close friends and mentors. Justin prayed and fasted, twice. Both of their hearts desired nothing but God's perfect will.

Despite living out a Holy Spirit directed life and keeping Christ at the center of their marriage, Justin and Renee have gone through very difficult periods and painful seasons in their marriage. But during these times, there was never any doubt our question in their minds whether the right decision was made to marry one another. The foundation of their marriage has not been shaken. They remain confident in what they heard the Lord speak to their hearts; that it was His will for them to marry. The more confident we are in walking out God's will, the more we communicate with Him, the less we will be shaken by fear and doubt from the enemies lies during times of conflict. This is the power of hearing the still, small voice of God.

INDIVIDUAL/GROUP DISCUSSION QUESTIONS

1. The Wholeness Equation is $1 + 1 = 3$. What is the missing variable in our relational equation that results in wholeness?
    1 (you) $+ 1$ (God) $+ \rule{2cm}{0.4pt} = 3$ (Wholeness) (p.119)

2. Why do we continually need to be filled with the Spirit? (Ephesians 4:30-31; p.120)
    _____
    _____
    _____
    _____

3. What are two ways to be filled with the Spirit? (Ephesians 5:18-20)
    _____
    _____
    _____
    _____

4. What does praying in the Spirit give God permission to do? (p.126)

_____
_____
_____
_____

5. How does effective prayer happen? (1 John 5:14; p.127)

_____
_____
_____
_____

6. What are some reasons praying in the Spirit is so powerful? (Romans 8:26, 1 Corinthians 2:16, 10-13, 14:2,14; p.129)

_____
_____
_____
_____

7. How do we take hold of the two-edged sword offensively? (p.130)

_____
_____
_____
_____

8. Why is giving thanks so powerful? (Matthew 14; Mark 6; Luke 9; John 6; p.131)

_____
_____
_____
_____

9. Why is thanking God an expression of humility? (Romans 4:4-5; p.132)

_____
_____
_____
_____

10. How does giving thanks make your faith effectual? (Philemon 1:6 KJV; p.133)

_____
_____
_____
_____

CHAPTER 9

NETWORK: THE POWER OF INFLUENCE

9.1 YOUR INNER CIRCLE

Now that we have established our beliefs in the truth of God's Word, we understand faith is what puts our beliefs into action giving substance to our identity. We know powerful ways to communicate with God, and we have the knowledge to live everyday life in God's presence or Rest. However, apart from ourselves, nothing has the ability to take us out of the presence of God faster than those we choose to surround ourselves with (Amos 3:3, 1 Corinthians 15:33).

For us to continue our cultivation of a life experiencing God's perfect love, it is imperative for our inner circle to be made up of those who not only understand the perfect love of God (Ephesians 3:19) but are also pursuing God's heart and passions on their own.

> Nothing has the ability to take us out of the presence of God faster than those whom we choose to surround ourselves with.

> *Proverbs 13:20 (NIV): Walk with the wise and become wise, for a companion of fools suffers harm.*

In Proverbs 13:20, the phrase "walk with" is Hebrew for "halak" (הָלַךְ), and means "to live", and is also figurative for "a manner in life". This verse is referring to the manner of life that is produced from walking with various people. Walking with some individuals will produce a life full of wisdom, others a life of foolishness. The Bible is speaking of the power of peer influence that our inner circle has on us.

The foundation of every social network starts with an inner circle. When speaking of our inner circle, I'm referring to the few, select individuals we choose to experience life with. It's a relatively generic term, as there is no standard or stereotype for those who typically consist of one's inner circle other than those we chose to be close to. And that is dangerous when we let anyone in.

The inner circle of some may include family members, for others it may not. For some, it is the people they work with or play sports with, for others it may be someone they have known since childhood. Simply speaking, our inner circle consists of those we choose to experience life with.

The core of our network, our inner circle, consists of the people we trust and confide in with the intimate and vulnerable details of life. It is those we choose to live everyday life with. People who are grounded and stable in God's Word are a wise choice for our inner circle (Proverbs 11:14, 12:15, 20:18). They are the ones we need to influence us. Thus, we will learn about the power of peer influence.

It is properly documented that science and the Bible acknowledge both the existence and power of peer influence. For example, the hypothesis (theory or idea) that children are influenced by their friends' attitudes and behaviors is hardly controversial. This hypothesis is found in the philosophical and religious writings of authors from thousands of years ago (Berndt & Murphy, 2002).

Despite the Word of God saying it exists combined with the acknowledgment of science, it is still relatively unknown why peer influence is so influential and powerful. This lack of knowledge in ascertaining the 'how' and 'why' of peer influence is attributed to the difficulty of developing research by creating practical, reliable, and valid methods to truly test, define, and convey the power of peer influence. In other words, it is difficult to objectively measure the influence our friends have on us. What we do know is peer influence starts early in life and as Proverbs 13:20 states, continues into adulthood. Let us understand why peer influence is so influential.

9.2 THE POWER OF PEER INFLUENCE

Leading the theoretical (thoughts or ideas) causes of peer influence are the processes of:

1. Reinforcement
2. Observational Learning
3. Information Exchange
4. Group Polarization

We will quickly address these concepts and see how they relate to one another, thereby theoretically causing the phenomena known as peer influence. As we briefly go over these causes of peer influence, see if you can recognize how any of these processes have taken place in your life and relationships.

1. **Reinforcement:** Boys that are high in antisocial behavior consistently exhibited positive responses at their friend's deviant behaviors, showing that the greater the reinforcement, such as the degree of laughing or other acts of positive reinforcement, the greater the escalation of the delinquent behaviors over time (Dishion, McCord, & Poulin, 1999; Dishion, Poulin, & Burraston, 2001; Dishion, Spracklen, Andrews, & Peterson, 1996).

The research of Dishon and colleagues confirms that friends do not need to pressure their friends to engage in behavior, but rather to simply make the behavior seem exciting and enjoyable (Berndt & Murphy, 2002).

This is reinforcement. I would like to think of it as a form of encouragement, and the greater reinforcement or encouragement the greater increase in the behavior, regardless of whether it's negative or positive.

2. **Observational Learning:** Relationships engage children in human community in ways that help them define who they are, what they can become, and how and why they are important to other people (Bornstein, 2002; Cassidy & Shaver, 1999; Cochran et al, 1990; Fogel, 1993; Rogoff,

1990; Shonkoff & Phillips, 2000; Thompson, 1998).

-- National Scientific Council on the Developing Child, 2004

Observational Learning is saying that children experience their world as an environment of relationships, and these relationships affect virtually all aspects of their development including our topic of self-worth. Relationships are the active ingredients of an environment's influence on healthy human development. They incorporate the qualities that best promote competence and well-being, individualized engagement and responsiveness, mutual action-and-interaction, and an emotional connection to another human being through relationships of any sort.

In more simpler words, we pick up on the behaviors of those we look up to, respect, and admire, so much that we can take on their characteristics as our own, allowing it to influence who we become (identity). One negative example of observational learning is when a friend sees another friend smoking a cigarette, and they choose to try one. A positive example is when a friend tells another friend they are going to read their Bible before bed, and as a result, they decide to do so as well.

3. **Information Exchange:** Despite social influence [information exchange or dialogue] among friends being a mutual process, such as individuals influencing their friends and their friends influencing them, the common result of the interaction of influence or information sharing, is that the characteristics of the individuals typically becomes more similar [or will harmonize] to the group (Savin-Williams & Berndt, 1990).

In other words, students who have friends who are higher in disruptive behavior will increase their disruptive behavior, and students who have friends who are lower in disruptive behavior will decrease their disruptive behavior (Berndt & Keefe, 1995) because the behaviors will harmonize. This is reinforced Biblically:

Amos 3:3 (KJV): Can two walk together, except they be agreed?

Amos is not saying that only people who agree with one another will walk together, but rather those who walk together will eventually come to the same beliefs. This is important because as we previously discussed, beliefs drive behavior. Those we choose to experience life with, our beliefs will eventually harmonize with one another and we will come into agreement. This is the reason 'missionary dating' or being unequally yoked is a very difficult situation to navigate. The longer the walk is or the longer the relationship, the more beliefs will harmonize due to information exchange.

4. **Group Polarization**: Isenberg (1986) defines group polarization as taking place when the initial tendency of individual group members toward a given direction is enhanced or dramatized following group discussion or information exchange (dialogue).

When the average beliefs of group members were biased, or 'polarized', in a given direction before discussion, the bias usually increased after discussion so that the final group decision [or beliefs] were more extreme, or radicalized, than the initial opinions of the individuals in the group prior to discussion (Berndt & Murphy, 2002).

To make sense of this, we will use an example of alcohol consumption. Group polarization would preclude that if we brought together a group of individuals who were moderate drinkers at home, by themselves, they would drink more excessively when together in a group. In other words, behaviors polarize or become more extreme. This is the reason many alcoholics can drink at home and cut it off after a few, even one, thinking they don't have a problem. In their perception, they are exercising control. However, when with friends at the bar they lose control and get intoxicated due to group polarization, and then make poor decisions, such as driving under the influence.

Their drinking becomes more extreme, or 'polarized', in a group setting due to peer influence. This also holds true concerning behaviors viewed as positive. People who workout in a group are more likely to meet goals when compared to those who workout alone.

Another example is if you take an individual who studies the Bible moderately at home while alone and you place them in a group Bible study, their passion for studying the Bible will increase, or polarize, while being in the group. This is the reason book clubs help people read books, and why Alcoholics Anonymous groups help people maintain sobriety, for example.

APPLICATION

Think of the phenomena of peer influence, reinforcement, observational learning, information exchange, and group polarization, and as you reflect on examples of how your friends have influenced your behavior, for better or worse, see if you can recall these principles taking place in life.

Also, think of areas that you want to improve in your life. Find people who are successful in those areas and ask them to be in your life. This is a form of mentoring and is effective because of peer influence.

Group polarization is also why youth camps and ministry conferences are so powerful. You take a group of youths or believers who are individually seeking God on their own and place them together for a weekend, their faith polarizes becoming more extreme, and they move mountains!

Group polarization is even mentioned in the Bible:

> Matthew 18:20 (KJV): For where two or three are gathered in my name, there am I in the midst of them.

There is one more component of peer influence I feel the need to address, and it is timing. An example of the influence of timing is a study which showed the influence of friends on their friends' educational aspirations increased between tenth and twelfth grade (Hallinan & Williams, 1990). This happened because decisions about college are more relevant to seniors in high school than to sophomores. Not only is the friendship there, but more importantly is the timing component. Friends talk more about college decisions (information exchange) in the twelfth grade than in the tenth grade, thereby having more influence on each other's decisions (Berndt & Murphy, 2002).

There are a couple of things going on in this study. First, the friends who were influential were in the inner circle. They held rapport and trust because of their history. This makes sense in the college example because as you contemplate a significant life decision, such as college or marriage, you will be selective in whom you seek counsel with, hopefully. Second, the timing (twelfth grade) was right for their discussions about college, therefore it bore the fruit of influence in decision-making. In contrast, the influence remained insignificant when discussed during the tenth grade. Timing matters.

> The people who will be there when the time is right, or wrong for that matter, are in our inner circle. What they say will influence us for better or worse because they will be present when we're vulnerable and in need of direction. We must choose our inner circle carefully.

The people who will be there when the time is right, or wrong for that matter, are in our inner circle. What they say will influence us, for better or worse, because they will be present when we're vulnerable and in need of direction. We must choose our inner circle carefully.

Proverbs 18:24 (NIV): One who has unreliable friends soon comes to ruin, but there is a friend who sticks closer than a brother.

Now that we have discussed peer influence scientifically through research, we will see its impact in the Word of God. We are going to look at two Biblical examples of peer influence: The story of Shadrach, Meshack, and Abendnego, and the four friends who lowered the paralyzed man through the roof in Capernaum.

In Daniel 3, Daniel was appointed ruler over the whole province of Babylon, which was under the control of King Nebuchadnezzar. Daniel, who found favor in King Nebuchadnezzar's eyes because he interpreted a dream, appointed Shadrach, Meshach, and Abednego as his assistants to help him rule over the provenance. Even unbelievers, such as King Nebuchadnezzar, can see when the hand of God is on a person's life!

King Nebuchadnezzar made a statue of gold attempting to unite the nation and solidify his throne by centralizing the worship of himself, more or less. He made a decree that upon hearing a certain song, everyone was to fall on their knees and bow down to worship an image of himself made of gold. Whoever did not do so would be thrown into the fiery furnace and burned alive.

Shadrach, Meshach, and Abednego chose not to worship the golden image of King Nebuchadnezzar because they served the one and true God Almighty. As a result, they were thrown into the fiery furnace. As you reflect on this story, don't focus on the fiery furnace but rather focus on the peer influence the three had on one another that fostered the courage to stand up for what they believed in, despite the dreaded outcome. I believe they were able to individually stand up to King Nebuchadnezzar in the face of death because they stood together. Can you imagine the discussion they must have had with one another? Their faith polarized as a group and defeated one of the greatest fears of man: Being burned alive.

> I believe they were able to individually stand-up to King Nebuchadnezzar in the face of death because they stood together.

It is crucial to have the right people around you, and it is very destructive to have the wrong people around you.

THINKING POINT

What do you think the group discussion was like between Shadrach, Meshach, and Abednego? How much do you think they reinforced one another to stand for their faith despite the threat of being burned alive? Do you think they would have been as righteously defiant to King Nebuchadnezzar if they would have been standing before him alone?

Another example of the power of peer influence is found in Mark 2, where a group of four men lowered their paralyzed friend through a roof down to Jesus.

> *Mark 2:4 (NIV): Since they could not get him to Jesus because of the crowd, they made an opening in the roof above Jesus by digging through it and then lowered the mat the man was lying on.*

People who do not have control of their body or independence (paralytics) experience a great deal of anxiety and fear when they know they are unstable. This is evident in my experience of lifting them from their wheelchair even a few feet from the ground to be placed on their bed. The main reason they are afraid is that they know that if something were to happen, if they were to fall, they are incapable of supporting or catching themselves. Falling even a few feet could be detrimental, even fatal, because of their inability to protect their bones and organs in their body.

Could you imagine what the paralytic was experiencing in Mark 2, when his friends told him they were going to lower him through a roof? He must have thought they were nuts! I can see the fear in his eyes, I can feel his body tense, I can hear his voice shake when asking his friends if they were sure this was a good idea.

If the story was told through the perspective of the paralytic, I could imagine as excited as he was to meet Jesus, his fear of being lowered through the roof was real and reason enough to doubt and hesitate following through with the plan.

I assure you with confidence, this plan of being lowered through the roof was not the idea of the paralytic. In fact, I believe this was why four men had to carry him rather than just two (Mark 2:3). I believe fear may have made him a bit reluctant.

The story of the paralytic is a story about the friends of the paralytic, not the paralytic himself. The paralytic was saved because of his belief and faith in Jesus Christ; he was healed because of the faith of his friends.

> *Mark 2:5 (KJV): When Jesus saw their faith, he said to the paralyzed man, "Son, your sins are forgiven."*

When Jesus saw their faith, He was referring to the faith of the four friends of the paralytic man.

The story of the paralytic is a story about the friends of the paralytic, not the paralytic himself. The paralytic was saved because of his belief and faith in Jesus Christ; he was healed because of the faith of his friends.

"Their" is not used to address one individual, but is plural, meaning more than one. We then know Mark differentiated the two because He recorded Jesus addressing the paralyzed man separately, after He addressed the faith of the friends.

The four friends were relentless in their pursuit of freedom and healing for their paralyzed friend. To place this in a greater perspective, we must remember during the time of Jesus, people who were sick and disabled were viewed very poorly by society. In fact, one of the beliefs of the Jewish culture was that if someone was born with a disease, disability, or experienced calamity or suffering in life, it was because of sin and it was a form of punishment from God. Unfortunately, some of us can still believe this inaccurate theology today.

> John 9:2 (KJV): And His disciples asked Him, saying, Master, who did sin, this man, or his parents, that he was born blind?

I am certain the four men were ridiculed as they lowered their friend through the roof; the crowd most likely thought it was pure foolishness. But they were determined because they were moved to action by an unconditional love that overflowed from their faith in Jesus Christ. This is the power and ability of our inner circle to bring us results in life. This is the power of the right kind of peer influence.

9.3 BAD INFLUENCES

In discussing examples of the benefits of having an inner circle that is established with Spirit-filled, godly men and women, we can understand the importance of eliminating bad influences.

Scientific research showed us that individuals would increase behaviors to conform to their inner circle, and the common behaviors or stances of the individuals within the group are radicalized, or polarized, as a group. Therefore, we can understand that if our inner circle consists of individuals who do not live for God, we will naturally gravitate towards a life that is not living for God as well. Not only will we gravitate to where they are in life, but as a group we will move towards or escalate in undesired behaviors to a greater level (group polarization).

> 1 Corinthians 15:33-34 (KJV): Be not deceived: evil communication corrupts good manners. (34) Awake to righteousness, and sin not; for some have not the knowledge of God.

As we see in 1 Corinthians 15, when we form our inner circle of friends, a factor in choosing our friends needs to be their knowledge or beliefs of God. This is not a generic knowledge, but an intimate knowledge of not only God's perfect love, but the gift of righteousness. If you remember, the Greek word used for "to know" God in Ephesians 3:19, is a Jewish idiom for sexual intercourse between a man and woman. It is an unveiling, a personal, intimate revelation (2 Corinthians 3:18) of God's peace and love that passes understanding (Philippians 4:7, Ephesians 3:19).

When we invite our friends to influence our choices and behaviors, we want to make sure they not only know God, but are also living in His peace and love. If our friends are aligned with the Word of God, their influence will be aligned to the Word as well, and we will reap the fruit of their wisdom, discernment, and the knowledge of God through their counsel.

Remember, two who walk together will harmonize their beliefs (Amos 3:3). If we walk with friends who have inaccurate beliefs about God, not only will it rub off on us, but we will begin to question God in the experiences we share with our friends. We will fail to receive the benefits of friends established in the perfect love of God.

By staying in God's Word and avoiding the thoughts, behaviors, and influences that He has healed us from, we can nurture and grow the healing He initiated, eventually reaping the fruit of wholeness.

It is crucial to our continued development in Christ to let go of bad influences. By staying in God's Word and avoiding the thoughts, behaviors and influences that are harmful to us and our relationship with God, we can nurture and grow the healing He initiated, eventually reaping the fruit of wholeness. God's Word is always healing us (Psalm 107:20). We fail to experience the full and complete manifestation of God's healing because we do not give it time to bear fruit. We fail to grow and nurture His healing when we return to what we are being healed from.

REAL LIFE

It is difficult for Justin to say there was anything 'tough' about his supernatural, overnight healing and change. When you go from a life of addiction, destruction, and torment to a life of God's perfect love and wholeness in a single night, realistically, how could it possibly be tough?

Despite the work God did in his heart, despite the healing and wholeness God purposed, despite the revelation he received of God's love and peace, the process of losing his friends was extremely difficult. Justin had to keep the door to those influence slammed shut to stay away from peer influence. He knew that going back to that circle of friends would have sucked him back into that destructive lifestyle. By slamming that door shut, God was able to continue the work He began in him.

The morning of his healing, he made a tough decision; he had to fall off the face of the earth. This decision had to be made without an explanation because he knew they would not understand. Many of them still do not today. How could one understand such a radical, supernatural, heart-level change that happened overnight?

Part of having the revelation of God's peace and love that passes understanding is the revelation of the deceitful and destructive power of sin.

When we disannul God's work through returning to previous thoughts and behaviors or environments and friends that are not in harmony with His Word, we wonder why we stop experiencing His perfect love or presence. It is not that He takes His hand off of us, but we reject what He has done by returning to what He has delivered us from (Proverbs 26:11, Matthew 12:45)

> When we disannul God's work through returning to previous thoughts and behaviors or environments and friends, we wonder why we stop experiencing His perfect love or presence.

9.4 CHOOSING CAREFULLY

Now that we understand the power of peer influence, discussed Biblical examples of the phenomenon, and understand why we need to eliminate bad influences, how do we make good decisions in relationships? The greatest way to choose our inner circle, whether it be friends or a significant other, is with a heart that is made whole, filled with the love and fullness of God (Ephesians 3:19).

Proverbs 12:26 (KJV): The righteous choose their friends carefully, but the way of the wicked leads them astray.

> The greatest way to choose our inner circle, whether it be friends or a significant other, is with a whole heart that is filled with the fullness of God.

One of the greatest reasons we make wrong decisions in friendships, especially in relationships, is because we make them with a heart that is not healed, made whole, fulfilled, and overflowing with the love of Christ.

> When we are healthy and full of God's love, our heart is satisfied and empowered to build healthy, life-giving friendships.

When we make decisions with a heart that is not whole, the choices we make are done to fill voids in our life, to try and mend a broken heart, or for a temporary fix. Whether we realize it or not, the choices are meant to numb the hurt and pain, or to be a distraction, rather than addressing the root of the brokenness. Choices made from a heart that is broken will lead to decisions that will result in a life that is broken.

When we are healthy and full of God's love, our heart is full and empowered to build healthy, life-giving friendships. When we are filled with the fullness of God, we will not settle or choose dysfunctional relationships to fill a need or void. We will not make decisions based on fear, but rather based on God's perfect love for us. We will not accept being treated poorly because we know our worth as a son or daughter of God. Healthy relationships are built when we understand that God is the one that fulfills us as a person; not people or even spouses. Therefore, we will be able to exhibit patience in choosing relationships carefully rather than making bad choices to feel a perverted sense of security or to self-medicate.

Proverbs 27:9 (NIV): Perfume and incense bring joy to the heart, and the pleasantness of a friend springs from their heartfelt advice.

Matthew 6:33 (KJV): But seek ye first the kingdom of God, and his righteousness; and all these things shall be added unto you.

9.5 YOUR MINISTRY

As we come towards the end of this chapter, you may realize I have yet to touch on the very subject of our network. Instead, I've shared scientific insight into how peer influence works, provided Biblical examples, explained the importance of eliminating bad-influences, and discussed how to carefully choose relationships with a whole heart. Now we are here.

When we begin to serve as the Holy Spirit leads us, our network will naturally grow with friends who not only genuinely care for us, but who share the same beliefs of a loving God as we do. This happens through fellowshipping.

When speaking of our network, we are talking about our inner circle of friends serving as the base or foundation of our life. Our network will naturally develop from this carefully chosen base that serves as our social foundation.

The greatest way to create this network, or our inner circle, is through friendships that are made while attending a church or ministry. Now, I am not merely talking about simply attending a church service and leaving without speaking a word to anyone expecting relationships to blossom. What I am referring to is finding a local church your heart connects with and planting yourself in it to grow and invest in not only your relationship with God, but in relationships with peers (Psalm 92:13).

I believe everyone should serve at a church or ministry in some form or another. Jesus was pretty specific in addressing serving (John 13:14-16). Having a ministry can simply mean a personal ministry such as at your workplace, school, or even those who are walking with you through a season of life. When we begin to serve as the Holy Spirit leads us, our network will naturally grow with friends who not only genuinely care for us, but who share the same beliefs of a loving God as we do. This happens in fellowshipping; spending time together with those who loves God.

Merriam-Webster defines "fellowship" as "a friendly relationship among people; the relationship of people who share interests or feelings; a group of people who have similar interests". The Greek word for "fellowship" is "koinōnia" (κοινωνία), and means, "joint participation", and comes from the root word "koinōnos" (κοινωνός), which means, "a partner, comrade, or companion".

To have fellowship means to participate in everyday life with a companion or partner. It is the group of people in our life that our heart connects with. When our heart connects with a group of people centered in on God's perfect love, an environment is created that enables us to experience the power of building healthy relationships. Building healthy relationships means love goes both ways. It means we share our ups and downs of life with those who share in our joys and mourn and pray during our struggles. We exemplify God's love by loving others, as well as receiving God's love through them.

Learning how to receive love or ministry from others is a way for us to practice receiving love from God himself. Remember, the most difficult part of a Christian's walk with God is simply letting Him love us without trying to earn it. We cannot love unless we have the love of Christ. We first need to receive it, and then we can exemplify it. And the greatest way we can show God's love is through serving others. Jesus clearly instructs us, through His example, to serve:

> *John 13:14-15 (KJV): If I then, your LORD and Master, have washed your feet; ye also ought to wash one another's feet. (15) For I have given you an example, that ye should do as I have done to you.*

We cannot love as Christ loves unless we have the love of Christ. We first need to receive it, and then we can exemplify it. And the greatest way we can show God's love is through serving others.

Think about this verse for a moment. If you had one final meal with your closest friends and family before you knew you were going to die, you would want it to be significant.

This would be your last opportunity to convey what is important to you and to show your love and appreciation for your friends and family. It would be a meal that would be remembered by them forever as it would be your last intimate moment together. This was the same for Jesus, and during this intimate time He chose to perform one of the most humbling and personal acts: He washed their feet, a significant symbol of servanthood.

During the time Jesus was on the earth, it was customary for the servants of the household to wash the feet of the guests of their master. They would often wear nothing but a towel on their waist, which is why Jesus took a towel and wrapped it around His waist as He washed and dried the feet of His disciples. In fact, He even washed the feet of Judas Iscariot, His betrayer. I believe the reason Jesus was able to wash the feet of the one who would betray Him, is that He was God's love in the flesh (John 1:14, 1 John 4:8).

If God in the flesh was willing to serve, as we mature and develop into the nature of God, our heart will naturally and joyfully desire to serve as He did. I am not saying serving will always be ideal or pleasurable. There are times when I have simply not wanted to serve because I was tired or grumpy. However, no matter the condition I had arrived in, I always left feeling blessed and in a better state. Love is powerful. Serving others is powerful.

When we serve others, it is God's love manifesting through us into the lives of those we are serving. Not only do they experience God's love through us, but we experience His love through serving.

When serving with a pure heart, serving will be life giving and will result in experiencing joy as the love of God manifests through us into others. This is the reason we are called to serve as Jesus did.

Just as washing the feet of His disciples was symbolic of the love Jesus had for them, when we serve others it is God's love manifesting through us into those we serve. Not only do they experience God's love through us, but we also experience

His love through serving. The more we get to know God intimately, the more being obedient to Him will be the most gratifying feeling on the planet. All the blessings and provision from obedience will just be a bonus.

This is the reason, contrary to popular belief, serving gives life rather than drains it. The more we live in God's Grace, the more serving will be a natural love of ours even when we do not 'feel' like it. Why? Not only because it exemplifies the perfect love of God, but because when we serve we are being blessed.

> *John 13:17 (KJV): If ye know these things, blessed are ye if you do them.*

Serving in ministry is where God matures and grows us through relationships and is a natural, organic way to develop a Christ-centered network through fellowshipping. Serving is another place, as well as being in God's presence, where we receive life when the struggles of life are overwhelming. It is where we are encouraged and strengthened by our peers through the Holy Spirit and prayer, together, that unleashes the glory of God in our life. Serving in ministry sharpens our mind along with the minds of our brothers and sisters in Christ (Proverbs 27:17). It is where our faith is challenged and developed.

> **Serving is another place, as well as being in God's presence, where we will receive life when the struggles of life are overwhelming.**

When we serve, God is not only in the midst of it for the benefit of the person we are serving, but also for *our* benefit and blessing as well. When we serve, we experience the favor of God as the rivers of life flow from inside of us to those around us. This overflow of God's love will carry into our everyday life.

This serving component of our network is vital in living a life of experiencing God's perfect love; of living everyday life in His presence.

> *Matthew 18:20 (KJV): For where two or three are gathered together in my name, there am I in the midst of them.*

REAL LIFE

Serving in ministry or at a church is not only a wonderful way to establish healthy friendships, but it is also a great way to grow and mature in Christ. When we serve and are placed in leadership positions, we will get asked some challenging questions by some very hurt people. Questions such as "Why did God take my child?" One woman approached Justin and Renee at the altar requesting prayer for her sister who lost some cognitive functioning due to a brain tumor. A week later she had a stroke, losing what functioning she had, becoming a vegetable, making her the primary caregiver of her sister. One can imagine the tough questions that may arise from these difficult experiences, or how hard it can be to keep hope in a loving God through these life-changing tragedies. No matter who we are, the heart piercing questions that come from living in a fallen world are difficult for anyone, let alone to a spiritually unstable individual.

Questions like these, over time, will cause individuals who are spiritually unstable to question their own faith and belief in God rather than utilizing the opportunity to nurture confidence in a loving God to others. When handled correctly, these circumstances, though deeply painful, can become catalysts for growth and development by seeking answers to our hearts cry not only in God's Word, but also through the pastors and leaders we serve.

INDIVIDUAL/GROUP DISCUSSION QUESTIONS

1. Why do we need to use wisdom and be cautious in who we let into our inner circle? (1 Corinthians 15:33, Amos 3:3, Proverbs 13:20; p.137)

_____
_____
_____
_____

2. Briefly use your own words to describe:
   Reinforcement:

   _____
   _____

   Observational Learning:

   _____
   _____

   Information Exchange:

   _____
   _____

   Group Polarization:

   _____
   _____

3. Explain the importance of understanding correctly Amos 3:3. (p.139)

   _____
   _____
   _____
   _____

4. Why is the story of the paralytic about the friends of the paralytic rather than the paralytic himself? (p.142)

_____

_____

_____

_____

5. What is the best tool to use to make healthy choices in relationships? (Ephesians 3:19; p.145)

_____

_____

_____

_____

6. Why is it crucial to serve at a church? (John 13:14-15; p.148)

_____

_____

_____

_____

CHAPTER 10

YOUR TRANSFORMATION

10.1 THE BATTLE OF THE MIND

At the beginning of this book we spoke about the five parts, or systems, of life that make up the whole. These systems are our Beliefs, Faith, Identity, Communication, and Network. The first three inner-systems of our life, Beliefs, Faith, and Identity, when combined, make up what the Bible calls our inner man (Ephesians 3:16).

This chapter will bring everything we have learned up until this point together in one place; our inner man. It is the place where life happens and, more importantly, where Christ resides in us through our spirit and the perfect love of God manifests. Our inner man is the very essence of who we are. This place, our inner being, is where everything in the Word of God and its' promises comes to life, manifesting into our everyday reality. It is the part of us that is empowered to live as Christ lived (John 4:17).

Our inner man is the place where the finished works of Christ are complete. Our inner man is the light shining in a world of darkness. Our inner man is where we glorify God; it is the place where His perfect love manifests through us into others. Our inner man is where God's Word comes to life, empowering us to exemplify God's peace and love that passes understanding. This manifestation of God's glory through our inner man happens in our transformation upon salvation. But most Christians really don't believe they have been transformed into the image of God.

To understand our transformation, we need to understand that our inner man is what makes up our very essence, or being, *spiritually* and not naturally. The spiritual and the natural are in conflict within us (Romans 7:15-20). We are a spirit in that we are created in the image of God (upon salvation), who has a soul (mind, will, and emotions), and lives in a body (John 4:24). Our spirit and soul compete with one

> We are a spirit in that we are created in the image of God (salvation), who has a soul (mind, will, and emotions), and lives in a body.

another to rule our beliefs, therefore reality, therefore life. Our body is what we use to function and interact in this realm through God's perfect gift of free will, and is subject to whichever we empower: Our spirit (righteousness) or our flesh (sin).

> *Galatians 5:17 (NIV): For the flesh desires what is contrary to the Spirit, and the Spirit what is contrary to the flesh. They are in conflict with each other, so that you are not to do whatever you want.*

Most Christians don't understand this battle between the flesh and Spirit, thinking this existing state of turmoil between righteousness and sin is something we just learn to live with. Then they learn to accept and live with this everyday struggle that contributes to an identity crisis: When behaviors don't line up with beliefs. When a Christian understands the difference between their spirit and flesh or soul, and the battle raging between the two, they will understand to live in the empowerment of the Spirit through renewing their mind to the Spirit and not the flesh (Romans 12:2). The result of this empowerment in the Spirit, by grace, is living as God sees us: Righteous (Titus 2:12, Philippians 2:13, 2 Corinthians 12:9). For the bondages of sin to be broken and to fully experience living in God's perfect love, we need to understand the battle between the Spirit and the flesh.

This battle between spirit and flesh, also known as warfare, takes place in our mind. The reason the outcome of this battle is important is that our body, therefore behavior, will follow whichever is dominant. Either our spirit will rule our being or our flesh along with the bondage of sin. Let us look at this Biblically:

> *2 Corinthians 10:4-5 (KJV): (For the weapons of our warfare are not carnal, but mighty through God to the pulling down of strong holds) (5) Casting down imaginations, and every high thing that exalteth itself against the knowledge of God, and bringing into captivity every thought to the obedience of Christ;*

This battle between spirit and flesh, also known as warfare, takes place in our mind. Our body, therefore behavior, will follow whichever is dominant.

The Greek translation:
"Carnal" is "*sarkikos*" (σαρκικός): "fleshy or having the nature of flesh".
"Pulling down" is "*kathairesis*" (καθαίρεσις): "to destroy or destruction".
"Strongholds" is "*ochyrōma*" (ὀχύρωμα): "arguments and reasoning; or beliefs".

2 Corinthians 10:4 is saying that the weapons of our warfare are not of a fleshy nature, or even spiritual in nature, but mighty through God [for] the destruction of inaccurate beliefs (thoughts). Let's look at the next verse and see why:

> *2 Corinthians 10:5 (KJV): Casting down imaginations, and every high thing that exalteth itself against the knowledge of God,*

"Imaginations" is the Greek word "logismos" (λογισμός), and means, "a reasoning or judgment hostile to the Christian faith". It is referring to inaccurate or "hostile" beliefs of God.

Every "high thing" is the Greek word "hypsōma" (ὕψωμα), and means, "barrier".

The context of spiritual warfare is over beliefs of truth and takes place in our mind or soul (the flesh). Inaccurate beliefs or "imaginations" are a barrier (hypsōma) between God and us because we cannot worship what we do not believe, and we cannot become what we do not believe in.

Inaccurate beliefs or "imaginations" are a barrier (hypsōma) between us and God because we cannot worship what we do not believe, and we cannot become what we do not believe in.

The thief comes to steal God's Word (knowledge of truth) from our minds and hearts, knowing it leads to destruction by becoming a barrier to God.

John 10:10 (NIV): The thief comes only to steal and kill and destroy; I have come that they may have life, and have it to the full.

Hosea 4:6 (NIV): My people are destroyed from lack of knowledge.

In stealing God's Word or truth from our minds, the enemy steals our identity in Christ. In other words, he keeps us from our transformation from a sinner to the righteousness of God (2 Corinthians 5:21). This is the reason God tells us to renew our minds, to remind ourselves of the truth of who we are in Christ and what he has accomplished *inside* our inner man—our new creation.

Romans 12:2 (NIV): Do not conform to the pattern of this world, but be transformed by the renewing of your mind.

Ephesians 4:22-24 (NIV): that, in reference to your former manner of life, you lay aside the old self, which is being corrupted in accordance with the lusts of deceit, (23) and that you be renewed in the spirit of your mind, (24) and put on the new self, which in the likeness of God has been created in righteousness and holiness of the truth...

Renewing our mind is crucial to living everyday life in God's perfect love. While living in a fallen world, we need to remind ourselves of not only the *truth* of God's loving nature and character, but also what Christ accomplished through our *spirit* in our inner man. The result of Christ's accomplishment is His completion of our transformation into God's righteousness through our resurrection in Him as a new creation. This relationship between our spirit and the truth of the Gospel is crucial in our ability to have relation with God. We see this in John 24:

John 4:23-24 (NIV): "But an hour is coming, and now is, when the true worshipers will worship the Father in spirit and truth; for such people the Father seeks to be His worshipers. (24) "God is spirit, and those who worship Him must worship in spirit and truth."

We need two things to worship God: A spirit and truth.

John 4:23-24 shows us that we need two things to worship God: A spirit and truth.

We have spent the last nine chapters learning about truth, specifically the truth of God's Word being His nature and character, as well as our identity as a new creation, spotless and blameless in Christ. This chapter will consist of learning about our spirit and that through our spirit we have been transformed into the image of God, resulting in our manifestation of God's glory.

1 John 4:17 (NIV): In this world we are like Jesus.

To understand the need to renew our mind to live out our transformation in Christ, we must understand the battle between the soul and Spirit that is within our very being. We need to understand this daily struggle that takes place within our mind, to be able to take hold of Christ's victory over the flesh. We will learn to take hold of our identity in Christ through being empowered by the Spirit, thus walking out our transformation in Christ. To begin this discussion, we will learn about the part of us that is in conflict with the Spirit: Our soul.

10.2 YOUR SOUL MAN

Our soul consists of our mind, will, and emotions. Some even include character and personality traits. Our soul is also known as our flesh or our carnal mind, describing our temporary states that change in contrast to our perfect, eternal, permanent, righteous standing in the Spirit (Romans 5:2).

*Romans 8:6-7 (KJV): For to be carnally minded is death; but to be spiritually minded is life and peace. (7) Because the carnal mind is enmity against God: for it is not subject to the **law of God**, neither indeed can be.*

The only way we have the ability to love as Christ loves is to love through the Spirit. Living in the Spirit is when the law is fulfilled in us.

What is the law of God?

John 13:34 (NIV): "A new command I give you: Love one another. As I have loved you, so you must love one another.

The only way we have the ability to love as Christ loves is to love through the Spirit. Living in the Spirit is when the law is fulfilled in us (Romans 8:4). Everything that Christ has given us has been given through the Spirit.

Romans 8:6-7 (KJV): For to be carnally minded is death: (7) Because the carnal mind is enmity against God:

APPLICATION

Carnality simply means anything that pertains to the five senses. For example, working out is a carnal activity, so is sports because it pertains to our five senses. What makes it sin is when we exalt these carnal experiences above the Word of God, such as when we derive our sense of worth by how good we are at sports, or lifting weights, for example.

To keep this from happening, we must keep our focus on God, worshiping Him in everything we do and acknowledging that it is only because of His goodness and Grace that we are who we are today.

When we place belief and trust in our flesh or carnal mind more than God's Word, it is sin.

Carnality simply means anything pertaining to the five senses (flesh). What makes carnality sin is when it is exalted above the Word of God; when we trust our five senses or the flesh more than God's Word.

Romans 14:23 (NIV): and everything that does not come from faith is sin.

This is the context of carnality that Paul is referring to regarding his sinful nature. It is our sinful nature to exalt our five senses, our carnal experiences above God and His Word. When we place belief and trust in our flesh or our carnal mind more than God's Word, it is sin.

Romans 7:23 (KJV): but I see another law at work in me, waging war against the law of my mind and making me a prisoner of the law of sin at work within me.

Romans 7 is a good chapter to see all the natural laws at work within our inner man. When Paul said, "another law at work in me," he was speaking of the law of carnality or flesh being at war with the law of the mind. In Romans 7:23, Paul speaks of the law of the mind and it simply means whatever we dwell on (or focus on) will manifest in life. In the Greek, it means "a rule of action prescribed by reason".

> We cannot do anything good or bad unless it becomes a thought first. This is why we are to seek God first in all we do, so our thoughts are constantly being aligned with His heart.

The action is behavior and the prescription of reason is referring to what focus or dwell on. Basically, behavior is prescribed by thoughts or beliefs. We cannot do anything good or bad unless it becomes a thought first. In other words, sin is a thought process. This is the reason we are called to seek God first in all we do so our thoughts are constantly aligned with His heart, making His passions ours (Matthew 6:33). Our thoughts are a prescription for behavior and if we dwell on them long enough, whether good or bad, they will become reality.

> *Proverbs 23:7 (KJV): For as he thinketh in his heart, so is he:*

> *Romans 7:23 (KJV): but I see another law at work in me, waging war against the law of my mind and making me a prisoner of the law of sin at work within me.*

In the same verse Paul mentioned a third law, the law of sin. The law of sin and death uses the law of the mind to take hold of the law of carnality. In other words, what we focus on (law of the mind) is what we will exalt and when it's the flesh or five senses (law of carnality), it will result in death (law of sin and death) because we are placing our belief and trust in the flesh (five senses) rather than God. The relationship between these three laws is the bondage of sin (Romans 6:6) or addiction and is not just in the context of drugs and alcohol. It includes the addiction to thoughts, therefore behaviors, that are rooted in fear and unbelief.

> What we focus on (law of the mind) is what we will exalt, and when it's the flesh or five senses (law of carnality), it results in death (law of sin and death) because we are placing our belief and trust in the flesh (five senses) rather than God.

Hebrews 3:12 (KJV): Take heed, brethren, lest there be in any of you an evil heart of unbelief, in departing from the living God.

The law of sin and death refers to the controlling nature of sin in that sin will hold us captive in the bondage and slavery to fleshy desires, or a carnal mind, resulting in death (Romans 6:23).

In this captivity, there is no fulfillment or peace but a constant struggle for something that can never be fulfilled. To me, lust is a good example. The world does not have the capability to fulfill our desires. Only God's love is fulfilling. This is the reason people who seem to have everything become alcoholics or drug addicts, even committing suicide.

When the Christian life 'isn't working', it is because the flesh or soul is dominating and hindering our empowerment in Christ through the Spirit. Power is defined as the ability to get results. When a Christian lacks results in their life with God, it is because they lack empowerment through the Holy Spirit from inaccurate beliefs.

This hindrance by the flesh is what causes us to feel 'distant' from God even though He is within us, with nothing able to separate us from His love (Romans 8:38-39). Much like grieving the Spirit with anger and malice, for example, we are spiritually insensitive to God when our soul or flesh has control over our body.

> Galatians 5:17 (NIV): For the flesh desires what is contrary to the Spirit, and the Spirit what is contrary to the flesh. They are in conflict with each other, so that you are not to do whatever you want.

> Romans 12:2 (NIV): Do not conform to the pattern of this world, but be transformed by the renewing of your mind.

Rather than living a life with the soul or flesh ruling our body through thoughts and feelings (carnal mind), transformation happens when the Spirit takes over and influences our soul (renewing the mind) and our body following.

Rather than living life with the soul or flesh ruling our body through thoughts and feelings (carnal mind), transformation happens when the Spirit takes over and influences our soul (renewing the mind) and our body following. The best way for transformation to happen is in renewing our mind to God's Word and what it says we are in Christ. If you remember, this is the essence of confession, which is speaking in agreement with what the Gospel of Grace says about us. This is also our offensive weapon in the double-edged sword, in that we are speaking God's Word over our essence or being.

The struggle, or battle, to live out our transformation in Christ, in a fallen world, takes place in our mind:

> Hebrews 4:12 (KJV): Let us labour therefore to enter into that rest, lest any man fall after the same example of unbelief (disobedience).

> Psalm 91:1 (KJV): He that dwelleth in the secret place of the most High shall abide under the shadow of the Almighty.

What is God's rest/secret place? It is His presence! In God's presence there is no fear or unbelief, but peace, confidence, and empowerment. It is the place where our inner man is strengthened to live as God has created us to live: Righteously!

Now that we have discussed our soul, we will discuss its opposition: Our spirit. This is the part of us that is one with the Holy Spirit. It is Christ-like (1 John 4:17), leading our soul and body into righteous-thinking, therefore righteous-living.

10.3 YOUR SPIRIT MAN

We are transformed upon salvation. Therefore, rather than our Christian life being full of striving to become Christ-like, life is a continuous journey of learning how to live out what we already are in Christ. Our life of righteousness is in continual opposition to our soul or flesh that we were born into in this fallen world. The conduit to our transformation from sinner to being Christ-like, the empowerment that we must take hold of daily

> Rather than our Christian life being full of striving to become Christ-like, life is a continuous journey of learning how to live out what we already are in Christ.

through a renewed mind to live Christ-like, is our spirit. To fully understand our spirit that is made one with the Holy Spirit upon salvation (Ephesians 2:15), we must return to the beginning of time.

Adam chose to eat from the tree of knowledge of good and evil. The result was death (Genesis 3:19). Not only did Adam die naturally, in the flesh, the day he ate of the forbidden fruit (Genesis 2:17 KJV), but he immediately died spiritually. And yes, Adam did die the day he ate of the fruit. To God, one day is to a thousand years and a thousand years is to one day (Psalm 90:4, 2 Peter 3:8). This is the reason no person in the Bible as ever, or will ever, live over a thousand years.

Spiritual death is what caused Adam to be cut off from God because of sin. This tangibly happened when he was cast from the Garden of Eden. This state of being spiritually dead is what we are born into in that we are born with a sinful nature. Most people believe we are born in God's image. Adam was born in God's image. We are not. We are born in the image of Adam (Genesis 5:3), in the sinful flesh. We cannot be born in God's image, perfect, Holy, and righteous, at the same time as being born with a sinful flesh. Two opposing realities, good and evil, cannot exist in the same domain just like darkness can't exist in light and light can't in darkness.

> Genesis 5:3 (NIV): When Adam had lived 130 years, he had a son in his own likeness, **in his own image**; and he named him Seth.

We are born in the image of God when we are 'born again' upon salvation. Being born again means our spirit comes to life when God breathes His breath of life into us (Genesis 2:7, John 20:22). The spirit is our new creation, meshed with the Holy Spirit, perfect and righteous, in perfect relation to God just as Adam was before he spiritually died from choosing to eat from the tree of knowledge of good and evil.

Before salvation, we are disconnected from God because He is a spirit and we are spiritually dead because we are born into sin or with a sinful flesh.

> John 3:5 (KJV): Jesus answered, verily, verily, I say unto thee, except a man be born of water and of the Spirit, he cannot enter into the kingdom of God.

John 3:5 states that we must be born of a spirit for salvation, or to enter the kingdom of God. When it says we need to be born of water, it is referring to the water or amniotic fluid of the mother that breaks just before delivery of the baby. This is saying we need to be human, not an angel or spirit, to be born again. Demons, for example, cannot receive salvation because they are not born of water.

This is also the reason demons hate water (Luke 11:24), as well as why Jesus cast the demons into the pigs and as dumb as pigs are, they were smart enough to jump into the water despite it costing them their life (Matthew 8:32).

> *John 20:22 (NIV): And with that he breathed on them and said, "Receive the Holy Spirit."*

In John 20:22, we see the salvation of the disciples. When Jesus breathed on them, He breathed life into their dead spirit. The phrase, "he breathed on", is "emphysaō" (ἐμφυσάω), and is the same meaning as the Hebrew translation of Genesis 2:7 that tells of God forming man from the dust of the earth, "breathing life" into his nostrils.

> *Ezekiel 36:26 (KJV): A new heart also will I give you, and a new spirit will I put within you:*

When we believe in Jesus Christ, we are connected to God through salvation because we are born a perfect spirit (Ezekiel 36:26 John 3:5) through being resurrected in Christ a new creation. Through Jesus, we spiritually come to life and have relationship with God through the Holy Spirit because the Holy Spirit and our new spirit become one (Ephesians 2:15). This is us being a new creation or re-born (John 3:3) and is the symbolism or meaning of baptism. It is also the meaning of us being the bride of Christ. Just as a man and woman become one flesh in marriage, we become one with Christ when our spirit 'marries' the Holy Spirit upon salvation.

> *2 Corinthians 5:16-17 (KJV): Wherefore henceforth know we no man after the flesh: yea, though we have known Christ after the flesh, yet now henceforth know we him no more. (17) Therefore if any man be in Christ, he is a new creature: old things are passed away; behold, all things are become new.*

When 2 Corinthians speaks of being a new creature, it is referring to us being a new spiritual being. "All things become new" is the new life that we have received that will last throughout eternity. We are not reformed or rehabilitated, but our life is recreated through our new and perfect spirit. We are literally given new life.

This is the reason when we are saved, we have the same habits, the same aches and pains, the same sickness or disease, the same voice, and the same hairstyle, for example. Our body stays the same and so does our soul. We are a new creation in our spirit, but our body and soul stay the same until the rapture (Matthew 24:42, John 14:3, 1 Thessalonians 4:17).

In the same verse, "old things passing away" is referring to the death of our sinful nature through God condemning it in the body of Christ (Romans 8:3). Now that we are connected to God in the spirit and have inherited the finished works of Jesus, we are made new, perfect, and righteous!

Our spirit is where we are made one with Christ. Our spirit that God breaths to life meshes with the Holy Spirit, and we become one (Ephesians 2:15):

> *Ephesians 2:12-16 (YLT): that*

Our spirit is where we are made one with Christ. Our spirit that God breaths to life meshes with the Holy Spirit, and we become one.

*ye were at that time apart from Christ, having been alienated
from the commonwealth of Israel, and strangers to the covenants of the
promise, having no hope, and without God, in the world; (13) and now, in
Christ Jesus, ye being once afar off became nigh in the blood of the
Christ, (14) for he is our peace, who did make both one, and the middle
wall of the enclosure did break down, (15) the enmity in his flesh, the law
of the commands in ordinances having done away, that the two he might
create in himself into one new man, making peace, (16) and might
reconcile both in one body to God through the cross, having slain the
enmity in it,*

It is our spirit that has been made perfect, that is enmeshed with the Holy Spirit as
one, and is what God sees when He looks at us in Christ.

*Hebrews 10:10 (NIV): And by that will, we have been made holy through
the sacrifice of the body of Jesus Christ once for all.*

*Hebrews 10:14 (YLT): for by one offering he hath perfected to the end
those sanctified;*

Perfection is needed to have a relationship with God. If there was darkness inside
of us, we could not have relationship with God. God cannot have a relationship with
darkness because He is the light, and we are children of the light
(1 Thessalonians 5:5). We have a problem believing that we are both perfect in
Christ and one with God because it goes against our logical, natural, fleshly
thinking. It is easier for us to identify with our behavior, because we can see it,
rather than our identity in Christ. But the truth is, we are both perfect in Christ and
one with God (Ephesians 2:15, 1 John 4:17).

*Deuteronomy 18:12-13 (NIV): "For whoever does these things is
detestable to the LORD; and because of these detestable things the
LORD your God will drive them out before you. (13) "You shall be
blameless before the LORD your God.*

*Deuteronomy 18:13 (KJV): Thou shalt be perfect **with** the LORD thy God.*

Being that our spirit is made alive and perfect upon salvation, it is through our spirit
that we connect to God through the Holy Spirit in worship, prayer, and communion.

*John 4:24 (NIV): God is spirit, and his worshipers must worship in the
Spirit and truth.*

Our spirit is also the source of our empowerment. Anytime God's Word speaks of
empowerment or being empowered, it is referring to being Spirit-filled (Isaiah 11:2,
32:15, Zechariah 4:6, Micah 3:8, Acts 6:8, 8:19, Luke 10:19, Revelation 11:3-6).

*Ephesians 3:16 (NIV): I pray that out of his glorious riches he may
strengthen you with power through his Spirit in your inner being,*

*Acts 1:8 (NIV): But you will receive power when the Holy Spirit comes
on you;*

Zechariah 4:6 (NIV): 'Not by might nor by power, but by my Spirit,' says the LORD Almighty.

The context of the Spirits power in us is evident through baptizing (Matthew 28:19), preaching the Gospel (Mark 16:15), victory (Luke 10:19), bearing witness (Luke 24:48), giving testimony (John 15:27, Revelation 12:11), fellowship (Acts 2:1), praying in the Spirit (Acts 2:4), resurrecting life (Acts 2:32), wonders and miracles (Acts 6:8), protection (Acts 8:1), laying of hands (Acts 8:19), judgment and strength (Micah 3:8), and spiritual gifts (Revelation 11:3-6, 1 Corinthians 12). This is our inheritance upon salvation. These are the fruits of the complete Gospel.

> *Matthew 6:33 (KJV): But seek ye first the kingdom of God, and his righteousness; and all these things shall be added unto you.*

Our spirit is not only the means to empowerment, but also our means to peace, the precursor to joy, fulfillment, fullness, pleasures, discernment, direction, and all the other inheritances we have in Christ.

> *Romans 8:6 (KJV): For to be carnally minded is death; but to be spiritually minded is life and peace.*

10.4 THE SPIRIT BARRIER

Now that we understand we are empowered through our spirit, and our soul or sinful flesh is in opposition to this empowerment, we can understand why the enemy wants to place a barrier between God and us. Because we are one with God, the enemy cannot place a barrier between us spiritually or physically. So, he tries to through our beliefs.

This is the reason in Romans 8:6, the barrier to the Spirit is to be carnally minded. A carnal mind is a mind that places more authority on the five senses, what we see, hear, feel, and experience, more than the authority of the Word of God. This barrier happens when we dwell in fear and disbelief; when we don't believe in God's faithfulness or don't believe God will do what He promises in His Word.

We see in Romans 8:3-4 that God destroyed the law of flesh through condemning it in the body of Christ. We see in Hebrews 9:26-28 that He appeased our wages for sin, which was death, in sending His Son to die for us as a perfect sacrifice.

> *Romans 8:3-4 (KJV): God sending his own Son in the likeness of sinful flesh, and for sin, condemned sin in the flesh: (4) That the righteousness of the law might be fulfilled in us, who walk not after the flesh, but after the Spirit (renewed focus).*

> *Hebrews 9:26-28 (NIV): But he has appeared once for all at the culmination of the ages to do away with sin by the sacrifice of himself. (27) Just as people are destined to die once, and after that to face judgment, (28) so Christ was sacrificed once to take away the sins of many; and he will appear a second time, not to bear sin, but to bring salvation to those who are waiting for him.*

If the law of the flesh and the law of sin and death have been defeated through the crucifixion of Christ, what is left to be a barrier between us and the Holy Spirit? The answer is the law of the mind and is why our mind is the battlefield for spiritual warfare. This is the reason God's Word tells us that our transformation happens through the renewing of our mind (Romans 12:2).

As we previously discussed, the Word of God says that the weapons of our warfare are not of a fleshy nature, or even spiritual in nature, but mighty through God [for] the destruction of inaccurate beliefs (2 Corinthians 10:4). This is because our inaccurate beliefs, or "imaginations", are a barrier (hypsōma) between God and us. We cannot worship what we do not believe, and we cannot become what we do not believe in (2 Corinthians 10:5).

> *Ephesians 4:22-24 (KJV): That ye put off concerning the former conversation the old man, which is corrupt according to the deceitful lusts; (23) And be renewed in the spirit of your mind; (24) And that ye put on the new man, which after God is created in righteousness and true holiness (identity).*

> *Romans 12:2 (NIV): And be not conformed to this world: but be ye transformed by the renewing of your mind,*

> *Ezekiel 36:27 (KJV): And I will put my Spirit within you, and cause (empower) you to walk in my statutes, and ye shall keep my judgments, and do them.*

The root of all sin is unbelief, not believing that the Word of God will do what it says it will do.

The reason our mind is the battlefield is because it is through our mind that thoughts and beliefs, when in opposition to God's Word, manifest as sin through behaviors. We see this in Colossians:

Colossians 1:21 (NIV): Once you were alienated from God and were enemies in your minds because of your evil behavior.

The root of all sin is unbelief--not believing the Word of God will do what it says it will do. This goes back to our faith discussion. Either we have faith, or we don't. Either we believe God will do what He has promised us, or we don't. Either we make decisions in life with a confident expectation of God's goodness, or we don't and we make bad decisions rooted in fear and unbelief.

> *Hebrews 3:12 (KJV): Take heed, brethren, lest there be in any of you an evil heart of unbelief, in departing from the living God.*

> *Romans 8:6-7 (KJV): For to be carnally minded is death; but to be spiritually minded is life and peace. (7) Because the carnal mind (fear/disbelief) is enmity against God: for it is not subject to the law of God, neither indeed can be.*

This is why right(eous) believing (a renewed mind) leads to right(eous) living (Proverbs 23:7).

When God gives us a heart of flesh upon salvation (Ezekiel 36:26), it is speaking of Him cleansing our conscience from guilt and fear, freeing our heart from the law of flesh and the law of sin and death. It is a pure heart that is sensitive to the Spirit. This is the reason we are dead to the law (Romans 7:4, Galatians 2:19), or dead to the sinful flesh (Romans 8:3, 13).

Remember, the law makes us conscience of sin (a guilty conscience), condemning and cursing us. A renewed mind does not focus on the world or fear, but places confidence (belief) in what God's Word has promised (faith), resulting in peace, joy, and righteousness through the empowerment of the Holy Spirit (Romans 14:17).

> *John 14:27 (NIV): Peace I leave with you; my peace I give you. I do not give to you as the world gives. Do not let your hearts be troubled and do not be afraid.*

> *Romans 8:6 (KJV): but to be spiritually minded is life and peace.*

Transforming into Christ's likeness manifests the glory of God through us by empowering us to love others as God loves us. It literally brings the Kingdom of God to this earthly realm (Romans 14:17). This is the very essence of being a light unto the world. This is not only why God commands us to love us as He does, but how He empowers us to do it through the Holy Spirit.

> *John 13:34 (NIV): "A new command I give you: Love one another. As I have loved you, so you must love one another.*

10.5 YOU ARE THE GLORY OF GOD

Many Christians who become saved don't realize the transformation that takes place within themselves. They don't understand that we have been made a new creation in Christ. The reason for this is the same reason that many of us, after years of being saved and reading our Bible, still don't live as who we fully are in Christ. We don't live empowered through the Holy Spirit. We may have been saved for years, but we don't live as a new creation, transformed in the image of Christ.

We continue to live with the same thoughts and behaviors (habits) as our old, dead, sinful nature that has been condemned and crucified with Christ. We still worry, live in fear and stress, and carry our cares rather than giving them to God. We strive to earn righteousness rather than freely accepting it, and therefore still try to earn God's love rather than freely receiving it. We continue to have an identity as a sinner rather than someone who was a sinner, saved by Grace, and made new in the likeness of Christ. We have a hard time believing we're God's glory.

To live out our transformation as the glory of God, we need to know it and we need to believe it. If you have read this book in its entirety, and more importantly the Word of God, you know it. Now you need to believe it because we live in a fallen world that entices us, on a daily basis, to live in the flesh.

The manifestation of our transformation happens when we renew our minds to the truth of God's Word, the Gospel of the Grace of God, and what it says about us (Colossians 1:22). Knowing and reminding ourselves of the Gospel enables us to worship God in spirit and truth (John 4:24). Through conquering our soul or flesh by living in the Spirit, we take hold of our empowerment to live as Christ lived in this world (1 John 4:17). We live out what we already are in Christ, which is righteous, thus becoming a living testament to the glory of God. This is the reason God's Word says you are the glory of God (John 17:22, 2 Corinthians 3:18).

So, how do we live out our transformation as the glory of God?

> *2 Corinthians 3:14-18 (NIV): But their minds were hardened; for until this very day at the reading of the old covenant the same veil remains unlifted, because it is removed in Christ. (15) But to this day whenever Moses is read, a veil lies over their heart; (16) but whenever a person turns to the LORD, the veil is taken away. (17) Now the LORD is the Spirit, and where the Spirit of the LORD is, there is liberty. (18) And we all, who with unveiled faces contemplate the Lord's glory, are being transformed into his image with ever-increasing glory, which comes from the Lord, who is the Spirit.*

2 Corinthians 3:14-18 compares the glory of the Old Testament, or the law, to the greater, superior glory of the New Testament, or Jesus. When it says, "that which is done away was glorious" (2 Corinthians 3:7-11), it is referring to the passing of the Old Covenant (the law) to the New Covenant, mediated by Christ in us through the Holy Spirit. It is through the New Covenant that we are empowered to fulfill the law through living a Holy Spirit-influenced life (Romans 8:4).

2 Corinthians 3:14 refers to people being blinded or veiled from remaining under the curse of the law (Galatians 3:13), meaning they are still conscious of sin or living in the flesh (Romans 7:5-6). They believe the only way they are justified or made righteous is through their 'works' or what they do, attempting to live 'good enough' to get to Heaven. In reality, they live in fear and unbelief because they do not know or believe what Christ accomplished on the Cross.

When it says in verse 15, "when Moses is read," it is speaking of those who are reading the Ten Commandments, believing they are called to live according to it perfectly to be justified or placed in right standing with God. This never works and is the reason why their faces are veiled. It means they do not have the revelation of Grace or God's perfect love. In other words, they do not believe that righteousness comes through faith and belief in Jesus Christ (Romans 3:22, Philippians 3:9).

My point in all this is to understand 2 Corinthians 3:18--the really good stuff!

> *2 Corinthians 3:18 (NIV): But we all, with unveiled face, beholding as in a mirror the glory of the LORD, are being transformed into the same image from glory to glory, just as from the LORD, the Spirit.*

When it says with an "open" or "unveiled" face, it is speaking of those who have the understanding or revelation that righteousness comes only through belief in Jesus Christ, rather than through obedience to the law of Moses (2 Corinthians 3:14).

The phrase "beholding as in a glass" is the Greek word "katoptrizō" (κατοπτρίζω), and means, "to look at one's self in a mirror". In fact, James 1 warns us not to walk away from the mirror and forget what we look like.

> *James 1:23-24 (NIV): Anyone who listens to the word but does not do*

*what it says, is like someone who looks at his face in a **mirror** (24) and, after looking at himself, goes away and immediately forgets what he looks like.*

What is the mirror that reflects our image as the glory of the LORD? The answer is the Word of God.

*2 Corinthians 3:18 (KJV): But we all, with open face beholding **as in a glass** the glory of the LORD,*

John 1:1 (NIV): In the beginning was the Word, and the Word was with God, and the Word was God.

> **When we read God's Word, we are seeing our reflection as God's image and likeness!**

The Word of God is God, just as Jesus was the Word made flesh (John 1:14). When it says, "beholding as in a glass the glory of the LORD," we can also translate it as "beholding as in a glass the Word of God." Here we see that the Word of God is a mirror or glass that reflects who we are in Christ, the glory of the LORD.

John 1:14 (KJV): And the Word was made flesh, and dwelt among us, (and we beheld his glory, the glory as of the only begotten of the Father,) full of grace and truth.

If the Word of God is a mirror reflecting God's glory (2 Corinthians 3:18), and the Word of God is God (John 1:1), and Jesus was the Word made flesh (John 1:14), what are we seeing as our reflection when we look in the mirror?

When we read God's Word, we are seeing our reflection as God's image and likeness! When we read God's Word and allow it to take root in our heart, we are being transformed from glory to glory, meaning we remind ourselves of not only who we are in Christ, but how God sees us! We remind ourselves that we are changed into the image and likeness of Jesus Christ, the glory of God through the Holy Spirit. Renewing our mind every day to the Gospel of Grace is critical to living out our transformation into the likeness of Christ.

Renewing our mind happens when we read and meditate on God's Word, allowing His Word to show us our reflection as His glory. We are being shown how God sees us. We must renew our mind so that we remember who we are in Christ, and so we can live everyday life in God's perfect love. When we receive God's perfect love, only then can we love those around us as God loves us, manifesting His glory into the world.

James 1:23-25 (KJV): Anyone who listens to the Word but does not do what it says is like someone who looks at his face in a mirror (24) and, after looking at himself, goes away and immediately forgets what he looks like. (25) But whoever looks intently into the perfect law that gives freedom, and continues in it—not forgetting what they have heard, but doing it— they will be blessed in what they do.

Good preaching shoves the mirror of God's Word in our face, reminding us that we are the glory of God in Christ! We are shown who we are when we hear the Gospel of Grace (Acts 20:24). Grace is the power of the Gospel of Jesus Christ (Romans 1:16) and, unfortunately, is not being preached enough today. When it is, sadly and too often, we exit the church service setting the mirror of the Word aside. We forget who we are by returning to a life of unbelief and fear (James 1:23), rather than living everyday life empowered through the Spirit.

> **Good preaching shoves the mirror of God's Word in our face, reminding us that we are the glory of God in Christ!**

The result of looking into the mirror of the Word of God and forgetting what we look like, is a life lived with Christ in frustration. We become frustrated in our walk with God when we hear the Word, we don't take it to heart, therefore the Word is not evident in our life (James 1:22). We are not experiencing the fruits of our faith.

THINKING POINT

Why do we try and change people through focusing on their behavior? Too many times we think that changing a person takes place when we get them to change their behavior first. This means that we are basing who they are from what they do. If God did this with us, we would be in serious trouble.

Being that righteousness comes from believing (Romans 3:22), why don't we think that we can change a person by showing them who they are in Christ, thus naturally resulting in a change of behavior?

The root of changing one's behavior or who they are, is through their transformation in Christ. This is the change that 2 Corinthians 3:18 is speaking of. When we show people who they are in Christ through God's Word, the mirror that reflects our glory in Christ, we will start to see results in those we invest in. Showing someone who they are in Christ is infinitely more productive than showing them what they are doing is wrong.

When we merely hear God's Word without engaging our heart, our soul becomes deceived and our heart begins to harden. The Holy Spirit is not able to bring God's peace, joy, and righteousness into everyday life. We return to our carnal mentality, thinking and doing life with our natural senses and effort rather than renewing our mind and walking out God's Word through living a Holy Spirit-influenced life.

> *Colossians 1:21-23 (NIV): Once you were alienated from God and were enemies in your minds because of your evil behavior. (22) But now he has reconciled you by Christ's physical body through death to present you holy in his sight, without blemish and free from accusation— (23) if you continue in your faith, established and firm, and do not move from the hope held out in the gospel.*

The Christian life is not a life of striving to get what we need from Christ. Christ's works are finished, meaning they're done and complete in us. There is nothing we can add to Christs' finished works. The Christian life is a life of learning how to live in Christ's completeness; learning to live as the Gospel of Grace says we are: Perfect and one with God.

> Philippians 1:6 (NIV): being confident of this, that he who began a good work in you will carry it on to completion until the day of Christ Jesus.

APPLICATION

Don't ever forget your reflection in God's Word; what you have been transformed into through the price of Christ's death. Don't ever forget when you look in the mirror, to see yourself as God sees you, without blemish.

Paul acknowledges that our transformation is learning to live out every day what we have already become in Christ. We read Philippians 3:12 as though our transformation has not yet happened, and then wonder why we can't break the bondages of sin in our life. Paul is saying that he is learning ("I may lay") through his pursuit of God how to live in what "*was* laid" or what he has *already* become in Christ.

> Philippians 3:12 (YLT): Not that I did already obtain, or have been already perfected; but I pursue, if also I may lay hold of that for which also I **was laid** hold of by the Christ Jesus;

Paul knew that life is learning to let God take control because it is through God's ability that we behave as we are in Christ, which is righteously. It is God who gives us grace, which empowers us to say no to ungodliness. And it is through grace that God works in us righteous behavior, not ourselves.

> Titus 2:11-12 (KJV): For the grace of God that bringeth salvation hath appeared to all men, (12) Teaching us that, denying ungodliness and worldly lusts, we should live soberly, righteously, and godly, in this present world;

> Philippians 2:12-13 (NIV): continue to work out your salvation with fear and trembling, (13) for it is **God who works** in you to will and to act in order to fulfill his good purpose.

We are already made perfect in Christ. The Christian life is not about striving to become, it's about learning to live in what we already are: Christ's perfection, the glory of the LORD. We have already been made perfect, we just need to learn through the Holy Spirit how to live out our Christ-like nature.

> Hebrews 10:14 (NIV): For by one sacrifice he **has made** perfect forever those who are **being made** holy.

So, how do we continue in the faith, becoming established and firm by learning to live in what we already are? The answer is in God's rest; it is in His presence.

> Psalm 119:105 (NIV): Your word is a lamp for my feet, a light on my path.

Psalm 16:11 (NIV): You make known to me the path of life; you will fill me with joy in your presence, with eternal pleasures at your right hand. Hebrews 4:11 (KJV): Let us labour therefore to enter into that rest, lest any man fall after the same example of unbelief.

The Christian life isn't about striving to become; it's about learning to live in what we already are: Christ's perfection, the glory of the LORD.

REAL LIFE

When Justin was supernaturally healed and transformed in a single night, God immersed His Holy Spirit upon him, like a cloud settling over his soul. Justin went to bed as an alcoholic bound by addictions and woke-up in God's peace and joy. His heart was made whole and pure. It was so evident that it seemed as if the behaviors of yesterday were but a distant memory of the past. He awoke as a new creation.

Justin desired more of God and nothing else. He saw life through the perception of God's love and nothing else mattered. Justin just knew that he was loved by God and that He was in control of his life. For the first time Justin experienced stability, and he literally did not do one thing to earn it.

In his transformation, Justin's heart went from a heart of stone, to a pure heart that desired God's presence (Ezekiel 36:26). He desired to learn the Truth about God. Justin desired to seek after Him and to know Him in everything he did. God not only caused his spirit to come to life, but He fulfilled the desires of Justin's flesh. The application of the Spirit in everyday life creates the confidence in Justin to know that when he seeks Him first, He will give him the desires of His heart. When Justin see's those desires manifest in his life, through faith, it only strengthens and emboldens his confidence in His love.

This confidence brings the peace in life that creates an environment for healing, joy, and fulfillment. We cannot experience God without being confident in Him; confidence is what creates an expectation of entering His presence at any moment or time during the day (Ephesians 3:12). This is seeking Him, and in His presence is the place where God can work in us (Philippians 2:13). In His presence is the fullness of joy. There are pleasures forevermore (Psalm 16:11)! This fullness of joy is experiencing God because no matter what we are going through in life, we can stand firm like Mount Zion by being confident in His presence, knowing His path for our life. This is **knowing** who God is. Knowing Him is knowing wholeness. Friends, this is salvation. This is grace. This is being saved, healed, delivered, prospered, protected, preserved, and made whole. This is the gift that we have freely inherited as a son or daughter in Christ: Grace.

INDIVIDUAL/GROUP DISCUSSION QUESTIONS

1. What two parts of our inner man are in conflict with one another, and what will the dominant one control? (Galatians 5:17)

2. What are two things that we need to worship God? (John 4:23-24)

3. What is the only thing the Bible tells us to work on or "labor" to do, and what is a critical factor of doing it? (Hebrews 4:12, Romans 12:2)

4. How are we made perfect? (Hebrews 10:14)

5. How are we empowered? (Ezekiel 36:27)

6. Define: (Romans 7:21-24, 8:6-8; p.155)
   Law of flesh (carnality):

   Law of the mind:

   Law of sin and death:

7. The "other law at work" in Romans 7:23 (KJV) is speaking of the law of flesh or carnality. How do the three laws work to keep us in bondage to sin (p.155)?

8. In being one with Christ, what part of us is made one with what part of God? (Ephesians 2:15; p.15)

_____

_____

_____

_____

9. How do we remind ourselves of who we are? (2 Corinthians 3:14-18; p.164)

_____

_____

_____

_____

10. What is our actual source for righteous behavior? (Titus 2:12, Philippians 2:12-13, 2 Corinthians 12:9)

_____

_____

_____

_____

11. Why is the Christian life about learning rather than striving? (Hebrews 10:14; p.166)

_____

_____

_____

_____

REFERENCES

Bateson, G. (1972). *Steps to an ecology of mind.* New York: Ballentine.
Berndt, T. J. & Keefe, K. (1995). Friends' Influence on Adolescents' Adjustment to School. *Child Development,* Vol. 66 (5), 1312-1329.
Berndt, T. J. & Murphy, L. M. (2002). Influences of friends and friendships: Myths, truths, and research recommendations. *Advances in Child Development and Behavior, 30,* 275-310.
Bornstein, Marc (Ed.) (2002). *Handbook of parenting (2nd ed.).* Mahwah, NJ: Lawrence Erlbaum Assoc.
Brooker, R. J. (2005). Genetics: Analysis and principles (2nd Edition). New York: McGraw-Hill.
Cassidy, J. & Shaver, P.R. (Eds.) (1999). *Handbook of attachment: Theory, research, and clinical applications (pp. 89-111).* New York: Guilford.
Cochran, M., Larner, M., Riley, D., Gunnarsson, L., & Henderson, C.R., Jr. (1990). *Extending families: The social networks of parents and their children.* New York: Cambridge University Press.
Dishon, T. J., McCord, J., & Poulin, F. (1999). When interventions harm: Peer groups and problem behavior. *American Psychologist, 54,* 755-764.
Dishon, T. J., Poulin, F., & Burraston, B. (2001). Peer group dynamics associated with iatrogenic effects in group interventions with high-risk young adolescents. In C. Erdley and D. W. Nangle (Eds.), *Damon's new directions in child development: The role of friendship in psychological adjustment* (pp. 79–92). San Francisco: Jossey–Bass.
Dishion, T. J., Spracklen, K. M., Andrews, D. W., & Patterson, G. R. (1996). Deviancy training in male adolescent friendships. *Behavior Therapy, 27,* 373–390.
Dispenza, D.C., Joe. "Evolve Your Brain: The Science of Changing Your Mind", 2007, p. 11.
Fogel, A. (1993). Developing through relationships: Origins of communication, self, and culture. Chicago: University of Chicago Press.
Griffith, J. L., Griffith, M. E., & Slovik, L. S. (1990). Mind-body problems in family therapy: Contrasting first- and second-order cybernetic approaches. *Family Process, 29,* 13-28.
Hallinan, M., & Williams, R. (1990). Students' Characteristics and the Peer-Influence Process. *Sociology of Education, 63*(2), 122-132.
Isenberg, D. J. (1986). Group Polarization: A critical review and meta-analysis. *Journal of Personality and Social Psychology, 50, 1141-1151.*
Kopf, S. (2002). *Jews rank high among winners of Nobel, but why not Israelis?* Retrieved from http://www.jweekly.com/article/full/18676/jews-rank-high-among-winners-of-nobel-but-why-not-israelis/
Lazarus, R. S. & Folkman, S. (1984). *Stress, Appraisal, and Coping.* New York, NY: Springer.
Lynn, C. D. (2009). Dissertation. *Glossolalia influences on stress response among Apostolic Pentecostals.* State University of New York at Albany. Retrieved from: http://gradworks.umi.com/33/66/3366121.html
National Scientific Council on the Developing Child. (2004). *Young children develop in an environment of relationships.* Working Paper No. 1. Retrieved from http://www.developingchild.net
Newberg, A. B., Wintering, N. A., Morgan, D., & Waldman, M. R. (2006). The

measurement of regional cerebral blood flow during glossolalia: A preliminary SPECT study. *Psychiatry Research: Neuroimaging*, 148 (2006), 67-71.

Peterson, C. R. (2011). *Medical Facts About Speaking in Tongues.* Retrieved From https://beingunderthenewcovenant.wordpress.com/2011/06/14 /medical-facts-about-speaking-in-tongues-%E2%80%93-carl-r-peterson-m-d/

Rosenblatt, P. C. (1994). *Metaphors of Family Systems Theory.* The Guilford Press. New York, NY.

Rogoff, B. (1990). Apprenticeship in thinking: Cognitive development in social context. New York: Oxford University Press.

Savin-Williams, R. C., and Berndt, T. J. (1990). Friendships and Peer Relations during Adolescence. In *At the Threshold: The Developing Adolescent,* ed.

Shonkoff, J.P., & Phillips, D. (Eds.) (2000). From neurons to neighborhoods: The science of early childhood development. Committee on Integrating the Science of Early Childhood Development.Washington, DC: National Academy Press.

Thompson, R.A. (1998). Early sociopersonality development. In W. Damon (Ed.), & N. Eisenberg (Vol. Ed.) Handbook of child psychology, Vol. 3: Social, emotional, and personality development. (5th ed., pp. 25-104). New York: John Wiley & Sons.

Watts, A. (1972). *The Book: On the Taboo Against Knowing Who You Are.* New York: Vintage.

Wrubel, J., Benner, P., & Lazarus, R. S. (1981). Social competence from the perspective of stress and coping. In J. Wine & M. Syme (Eds.), *Social Competence.* New York: Guilford.

Made in the USA
Lexington, KY
23 June 2018